Praise for Letters to Daniel

"Inner wisdom and the power of the Spirit shines in Deb Yoder's story of her relationship to her son through their heart-rending journey. Deb's honesty in writing her story as well as her son's story takes incredible courage and vulnerability. This book is a gift to a world where many families grapple with the effects of addictions and violence in its many forms. My life has been dedicated to inviting hundreds of people to explore the power of their own story, to take the inner journey of embracing "who I really am" with my shadow and my light, my wounds and my gifts. Deb Yoder's story is a masterpiece exemplifying the depth of that inner journey. Thank you, Deb. Thank you, Daniel. Your story offers hope to each of us who are willing to take our own inner journey. May the Spirit of God continue to be your guiding light."

— **Elaine Sullivan**, LMFT, LPC,
Mentor and Trainer for the Parker Palmer Work

"Dr. Deb Yoder is no stranger to struggle. She has persevered through a history of uncertainty, broken relationships, and fear. She pressed past it to embrace an authentic faith that made sense of her own life experiences. This is what makes *Letters to Daniel* so powerful. The words are not just sound advice but the vulnerable dialogue between a son and mom in struggle. This book is an invitation to witness the transformation of their pain into healing and wisdom. These pages contain the very lessons that nurtured her own son in his journey to wholeness. I urge you to read Dr. Yoder's challenging words where she offers great hope, equipping the reader to cultivate a strong, God-honoring life and hopeful future."

— **Susan Peters**, MA, UnBound, National Director

"*Letters to Daniel* is a story of redemption, but the path to getting there as revealed in this son and mother's story is full of heartache and uncertainty for them, and for all those who love them. Yet if there is a recurring theme, it is a mother's endless belief in her son, a refusal to quit on him inspired by her belief in an unrelenting, endlessly loving and forgiving God who never quits on us, a belief that nothing and no one is ever beyond God's transforming reach. Mother Deb's full love for God and for Daniel comes through line by line. I am rooting for all of us in our grace-filled journeys of living into our God-given wholeness. Thank you AND Daniel so much for finding the courage to share your story. A must-read for every person who desires to know God more fully, and especially for those and their families who are bound by addiction and without hope. A book about being "all-in" with God, for a life of true freedom and abundance."

— **Reverend Barb Harris**, MDiv., BCC,
former editor in chief, *Shape* magazine

"Choose life," says Moses to the Hebrews on the brink of the Promised Land (Deut. 30:19). "Choose life," says Deb Yoder to her precious, incarcerated son, Daniel. "Choose life," she says to us, her readers. In this beautifully expressed collection of letters, a mother's bared heart teaches her son—and us—

how to choose Life. The reader will walk away from this book with a profound sense of the love of God, and empowerment for entering a redemptive life of forgiveness, freedom, and joy, alongside her son."

— **Debbie Nichols**, Philosophy Professor

"*Letters to Daniel* is not just an amazing story of a mother loving her son, but it is a counselor that shows you a path out of chaos."

— **Byron M. Gillory III**, Director of
Reasonable Faith, Wylie Chapter

"Dr. Deb Yoder's courageous and heart wrenching story of her son Daniel's difficult journey touched my heart deeply. I admire Deb and Daniel for their courage in going public and their willingness to share in the hope that their story might be of use to others. Deb's voice—and her lens from the inside as a parent and the outside as a psychologist and Courage Facilitator—adds special value to this powerful memoir."

— **Dr. Sally Z. Hare**, President, Still Learning, Inc.
and Courage & Renewal facilitator

"Dr. Deb Yoder takes the reader on a journey of the power of faith while raising her son. I was captured by her gentle voice as writer, mother, and teacher. This inspirational book is a must read for any mother going through challenges raising her children or even questioning her own self-worth as a parent. I stand in awe of the brutally honest conversations between a mother and son. Together, they stood the test of determination, courage, and the majesty of loving, not just each other, but of trusting God. As a Christian and a parent, I was completely engaged and moved, even challenged, to begin praying more specifically for my own children and grandchildren. I wholeheartedly recommend this book and pray it reaches and touches the people who need it. I've been blessed by reading it."

— **Cathy Edwards**, M.S., Director
Community Relations, Mountain View College

"Walking with Debby through forty-five years of God's refining, I witnessed first-hand her struggle with life's adversity and in particular with her son, Daniel. I observed Debby live the Daniel journey before these letters were written. To see them in print is a strong reminder of the place to which God has led her. She moved from a confused seventeen-year-old to the woman, the author of these letters to Daniel, whose confidence centers itself in the knowledge of God's grace and love. As you walk with Deb through this journey encouraging the incarcerated, angry, blaming-others Daniel to the Daniel he is now, my strong belief is you will be encouraged in your journey through suffering."

— **Jane Robinson, Educator,** Co-founder and Director
of the USA Basque Student Summer Exchange

LETTERS
TO
DANIEL

The path out of chaos and into a life you love

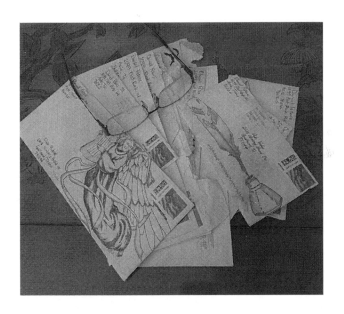

Debra M. Yoder

Harvest Works, LLC™

Letters to Daniel: The path out of chaos and into a life you love
by Debra M. Yoder

Cover and interior design by Nick Zelinger, NZ Graphics
Author photo by Jake Wangner
Photo of Daniel and Cora by Byron Gillory, Jr.
Cover photo by Deb Yoder/artwork on letters by Daniel Peters

ISBN 978-1-7337336-0-1 (print paperback)
Library of Congress Cataloging-in-Publication Data LCCN 2019901837
Yoder, Debra M.
    Letters to Daniel: The path out of chaos into a life you love /
    Debra M. Yoder
    1 spiritual life

Harvest Works, LLC™

To Daniel

Your courage to lean in to discomfort and chaos,
to challenge your own thinking, to discover
your true self—your highest, best, sacred self—is astonishing.
Your courage and vulnerability in sharing your story
will help others find their way out of chaos
into a life they love.
I love you forevers and always.

CONTENTS

Foreword 11

Introduction. 13

PART ONE: BECOMING AWARE 21
Teach me "Who am I?"
Chapter 1   The Power of Story 23
Chapter 2   Grasping for Hope 37
Chapter 3   Identity. 49

PART TWO: BECOMING MINDFUL 65
Teach me to think "How do I fix my broken life?"
Chapter 4   Thoughts and Words 67
Chapter 5   Emotions 79
Chapter 6   Faith 109
Chapter 7   Boundaries 130
Chapter 8   Presence. 137

PART THREE: BECOMING WISE 147
Teach me to change "How do I create a life I love?"
Chapter 9   Spiritual Formation 149
Chapter 10   Love 159
Epilogue   by Daniel Peters & Deb Yoder 165
Endnotes 173
Acknowledgments. 177
About the Author 179

Living the life we were meant to live doesn't just happen.
Success requires being aware of the inner self
and then mindfully applying strategies to bring
out the highest, best, sacred, real self.

~ Debra M. Yoder

FOREWORD

Dear Reader,

You hold in your hands a mother's heart, a heart stripped of any pretense or notion of perfection. A heart weathered by storms of heartbreak, struggle, disappointment, and shame so fierce at times she was unsure of her course. A heart beating in the soul of a courageous, grace-filled, hope-filled mother who would petition her God unceasingly for the life of her precious son, Daniel. A mother's heart laid bare again and again in written conversation with Daniel. A heart humbled by life yet held firm and secure in hope's healing powers.

In her latest book, *Almost Everything*, Anne Lamott[1] writes, "We are who we love, we are one, and we are autonomous. Love has bridged the high-rises of despair we were about to fall between. Love has been a penlight in the blackest, bleakest night. Love has been a wild animal, a poultice, a dinghy, a coat. Love is why we have hope." You hold in your hands the story of a mother's heart whose love bridges the distance between mother and son, brokenness and healing, death and rebirth.

In her role as Professor of Psychology at Mountain View College, Deb Yoder is unequalled in her graceful determination to hold space for students' toughest emotions, to provide guidance, compassion, and empathy, and to lead by example in the pursuit of lifelong learning. I was privileged to meet Deb during her recent facilitator certification process with Brené Brown's The Daring Way™ organization. I humbly and gratefully served as her consultant, all the while knowing I was being gifted the opportunity to learn from a master. We grew to become friends as well as colleagues in sharing our mutual passion and commitment to living life "all in."

As our connection deepened, I began to hear the life stories that have shaped this dedicated woman. She shares these stories in the pages that follow with courage and vulnerability, generously giving the reader full access to the pain and process of falling hard and rising strong again and again. Because I have been honored to walk beside her as friend, colleague, and fellow believer, I can wholeheartedly say that Deb values faith, family, and friendship above all else. She rests deeply in the love of her Creator, and fights fiercely for those she loves.

We must also share deep gratitude to Daniel for allowing his story to be shared with unflinching honesty. This is not only Deb's story, but Daniel's as well. It is also our story because it is the story of life. Life is hard and wonderful. Life is painful and joyful. Life takes our breath away, then gently and gracefully reminds us to be excessively gentle with our own hearts and the hearts of all others.

With gratitude,
Jeanye Mercer, MS, LPC, CDWF+ Consultant

INTRODUCTION

What I am looking for is not out there, it is in me.
~ Hellen Keller

WHO AM I? WHY AM I HERE?

"Teach me how to do life. Show me what I do not know. There has to be a better way to live. There has to be a more pleasant way to be in the world." These were so often my unspoken yearnings and sometimes my actual words screaming from deep in my belly out in to the universe. "Somebody, teach me how to do life!" This book is for those of you who may feel like that. It is for those of you who have sons or daughters or loved ones who do not seem to know how to do life well; for those whose lives are less than what you dream of; for those whose life is spiraling downward rather than getting better.

I believe in the power of story. The real and raw, true story. *Letters to Daniel* is the story of how I found my way out of chaos in to a life I love. I needed practical teaching. I needed to know what to think, to do, and how to be. I needed wisdom for living. I needed to know how to help my son. Perhaps you do, too.

This story is in three parts. Part one is *Teach me: "Who am I?"* It is about becoming aware; practical ways to explore your own story, grasping for hope, and discovering your true identity. Part two is *Teach me to think: "How do I fix my broken life?"* It is about becoming mindful; practical ways to manage your thoughts, your words, and your emotions; establishing what you believe, how to set healthy boundaries, and practicing presence. Part three is Teach me to change: "How do I create a life I love?" It is about becoming wise. We are either forming or deforming. What are the principles and practices of healthy formation? What is love? How do I create a life of joy and excellence?

I am absolutely convinced that no matter how messed up a life is, that there is a way out and up. There is a way, a path, ways of being and doing, that will lift a person out of chaos and allow them to do what my three-year-old granddaughter did the other day. She ran through the house with her hands up in the air in pure delight saying, "My life just keeps getting better and better and better!"

At the encouragement of a dear friend, I recently wrote a letter to my younger self. Now, at age sixty-three and looking back, I am truly amazed. Here is what my older self wanted to tell my six-year-old self:

"I want to tell you, precious, that everything works out in the end. I know you may be so shy and unsure now, but you will be amazed and delighted with how your life turns out. Hang in there. Keep breathing. Do your best. You do not have to have it all figured out. I want you to know that you are enough. You have access to everything you need to be successful to live and to love well. You will be loved. You will go places you never dreamed of. You will laugh until your belly hurts. You will give out of your abundance."

My younger self had no idea that there would be a thread woven throughout my whole life to anchor my soul. This thread, this truth, this anchor would hold me true to a path that was orchestrated for me by some unseen hand through uncertainty, self-deprecation, unworthiness, bad decisions, good decisions, failed relationships, heartache, desperation, delight, and a son who would bring me both unfathomable anguish and incredible joy.

This thread held me together when I was terribly unaware. With voices clamoring in my head telling me that I did not belong, that I had to earn my place in the world with no idea how to do that, shouting shame, whispering accusations, threatening to expose my worthlessness, I just kept breathing. Deep within me, there was this faint hope that there was a purpose for my being. There was an indistinct *knowing* that it was possible that my life could bring some good.

Looking back now, a half century later, I can see that love held me even when I rebelled and squirmed to go my own way. Looking back now, what foolishness there was in my heart, what arrogance in my head, that I could ever think that I could do life without the Life Giver.

"Rest." That's what I hear as I write these words. There is much talk about the "quality of life" these days, but the truth is that too many people are working too hard to create an ill-defined "life" in the future. We complain of being burned out, tired and frustrated, in-debt, lonely and suffering under the deadly effects of chronic stress, often without our being aware of it. We numb our discomfort by doing too much, drinking too much, eating too much, and either raging on others or raging on ourselves.

There is a much better way to be.

1995-2005

Life was beautiful. Two months before my fortieth birthday, Daniel was born, my one and only child. I had no idea what depth of joy was possible until I held him. Clear blue eyes, a mind of his own, an enchanting sense of humor, curiosity, and a love for cuddling with mom made the first few years a pure delight. Tee ball, learning to swim, and peewee football brought laughter and delight. When Daniel was barely three years old, we were in the car returning from a visit with grandma.

Behind me in his car seat, he said gently, "I've got birds in my pocket."

I laughed and said softly, "You do not have birds in your pocket."

"Yes, I do mom. I've got birds in my pocket."

How cute of this gentle little boy to imagine he had birds in his pocket. Now home, standing in the kitchen, he said it again so softly,

"Mom, I've got birds in my pocket." I smiled and reached down to his tiny blue jeans and patted his little pocket,

"You don't have...oh my!" He reached in and pulled out a handful of newly born translucent baby birds! He did have birds in his pocket! Daniel loved those tiny little baby birds, but I explained that they needed to go back to their mother. After some convincing, he agreed, and we drove back to grandma's house.

A couple of years later, Daniel came to me frantic, saying he could not find Duke, our miniature dachshund. We walked the neighborhood and the field surrounding the golf course across the street. When it got dark, we grabbed flashlights and drove the alleys, but there was no sign of Duke. Daniel's shoulders drooped as he hung his head in sorrow and worry. I told him we would pray for Duke, pray that someone would find him and bring him home. The next morning, Daniel still hung his head over his bowl of oatmeal before school. He was so very sad. Then all of sudden, he jumped up and yelled, "Mom! Get in the car! I know where Duke is!" Daniel instructed me to drive up the street to the golf course. Just as the sun was coming up, I pulled into the parking lot and Daniel jumped out and ran behind the building. A few minutes later, he appeared carrying a shaking, shivering Duke. Grieving over his oatmeal, Daniel remembered he had to hook Duke by his leash to the chain link fence so that he could go into the clubhouse to sell school fundraiser candy to the old men inside. He forgot to retrieve Duke and the poor tiny dog shivered through the night.

There were many joyful days ahead, but by the time Daniel was in fifth grade, his gentle eyes turned angry, and I did not know why.

The next ten years were quite challenging.

2016

At age twenty-one, Daniel's life hit an all-time low. How in the world can I help him now? A desperate search for answers drove me to dig deep and look at my own life. In my thirties, my life had hit an all-time low. Anxiety and depression were almost a constant. I hustled for significance through perform-ance and perfectionism; earning another degree or getting a promotion on the job did little to fill the gnawing sense that there must be more to life than this. Outwardly it appeared I was successful, but I knew something vital was missing. This book is an accounting of my search for answers to help Daniel, and in that process, life lessons emerged from my own experiences of falling and getting back up that I believe may be universal truths. Whatever you may be struggling with personally, or if you are searching for ways to help someone else, my hope is that my journey with Daniel will lead you to a path toward wholeness. Ultimately, it is a search for wisdom: *teach me how to live.*

It occurred to me that in all my letters to my son there was an urgency to pour into him any bit of wisdom gained over my sixty-three years. My hope was that he could be spared further heartache and be equipped to live a life of joy and excellence. Part of me feels a bit presumptuous to think I have something meaningful to share that can significantly help him along his way. But . . . another part of me trusts that my motives are pure, that love matters, and if I put my trust in the spirit of truth in me, that these imperfect but heartfelt words will indeed help set him on a good path.

In reading Daniel's letters to me, first from jail and then from Adult/Teen Challenge[2], I can see him progressively—in each letter—growing in wisdom. I am encouraged that the anger has subsided. He has a peace that draws others to him. I see patience and a sense of gratitude in him that was not always apparent when he was growing up. Peace, patience, and gratitude are gifts that extraordinarily improve the quality of a person's life. I was overwhelmed with joy to see his smile and feel his sincere hug when I visited him last Thursday.

The path toward wisdom often begins with a fall. Some never get up from a fall. They passively accept whatever happened to them as the final verdict. Others cry out for a new way to live when the way they have been living doesn't work. The first step out of the chaos is becoming aware. We become aware that we are not happy, or we fail time after time in relationships, or we hate our jobs, or we end up lonely, angry, or in jail, as Daniel did. Open your eyes to see, observe, that there is a better way to be in the world. Awareness comes when we observe others and ourselves: I mean *really closely observe*. Take a step back and see from a different perspective. What are you sensing? What are you feeling? Get curious about your observations and feelings. Making sense of them will come later, but first just observe, watch, feel what you feel, and get curious. If you press in and don't quit when it is uncomfortable or shameful, you will take the next step toward wisdom, becoming mindful. Mindfulness is being fully present with your thoughts and feelings. Think about what you are thinking. Lean into the feelings and don't run from them. Stay curious. Becoming mindful gives us the ability to see and understand the inner nature of things. We gain insight, intuition, and discernment. Mindfulness will bring understanding that will open the path toward wisdom. With wisdom, we know how to live. We have a skill set, a mindset, and the foresight to live in an intuitive flow with sound judgment. Life becomes easier when we grow in wisdom.

Perhaps now at sixty-three, thoroughly humbled, with compassion born out of brokenness, with no will nor right to judge another, empty of ego, silenced by shame, I say the very same words I said at age twenty-nine in a similar state of being: "God, if you are there, take my life and do something good with it because I sure have made a mess of things."

May these words—these letters—help you find your way out of chaos and into a life of joy and excellence.

Wholeheartedly for you,

Deb

PART 1

BECOMING AWARE

Who am I?

CHAPTER
1

THE POWER OF STORY

*A good journey begins with knowing where we are
and being willing to go somewhere else.*
~ Richard Rohr

It made no sense. My son's roommate, Terry, called me and said, "You're not going to want to hear this." I had no idea what was coming. My mind raced with the dark possibilities of what I was about to hear. After a long pause he said, "Daniel robbed a store. Aggravated robbery. He's in jail."

What? My thoughts were spinning. How could he do such a thing? Who does that? My one and only son, now twenty-one, the boy who was dedicated to God, prayed for all his life, dedicated in the church as an infant. I had declared over him, "Daniel is a man of peace, a man like Enoch who pleases God. Great will be his peace. He is a peacemaker."

Anything but! Daniel was an extremely challenging boy to raise. Besides his rages and explosive temper tantrums, he was always drawn to unsavory friends rather than the "good" kids in the neighborhood. He was violent and disrespectful to me and had spoken such hurtful words. I was astounded that he could know to say the most utterly vile things that cut to the core of my very being. When he was a young child, during rage episodes, I often had to hold him to keep him from hurting me or himself, until both of us were dripping with sweat and our muscles ached. Until he was twelve years old, I was stronger than he was, and it worked: I held him tightly until he went limp with exhaustion. Upon waking, he would cry and apologize profusely, snuggling in my lap and soaking in my comfort. Doctors had no answers. Pastors had no answers. Simple rebellion? Oppositional defiant disorder? Somebody help me! Help him! There must be an answer. He is suffering. I am suffering.

Special schools, counseling, a full psychological work up, all said he was perfectly normal. One psychologist said Daniel had above average intelligence and was angry at his dad's abandonment. Okay, so now what? My love, my devotion to him, counseling, providing the best possible environment I could with the resources I had -- nothing seemed to do any good. Although there were short periods of laughter, joy, and normalcy, it never lasted long.

Ironically, I am a professional counselor and psychology professor. For over forty years, hundreds of students have responded to my encouragement and mentoring with gratitude. Many have said I helped save their lives. Why can't I save my own son?

I wracked my brain to find solutions, explanations, treatments, the right structure, love and logic—all left me clueless. I begged God. I declared God's Word over him. When living with him became impossible, I sent him to my brother in California. If anybody could reach Daniel, my brother David could. Within a couple of months, despite David's sacrifice, love, provision, and dedication to him, David called me and said he could not live like this anymore. Daniel was violent, tearing up his house, speaking vile things to him, and rejecting every effort to find a solution.

I very nearly lost my job after getting several calls a day from Daniel's school telling me he had kicked the principal or gotten into another fight. Desperate, I agreed to let him go live with his dad. That did not go well. Daniel ended up in alternative school, started smoking marijuana, and fought with his also very angry dad.

At eighteen, Daniel seemed to be doing better. He had a job, a wonderful girlfriend, Morgen, and a beautiful baby daughter, Cora, whom he adored. I helped both him and Morgen enroll in college, and it seemed they were on their way. Again, hope was short lived. Irresponsibility, drinking, and anger cost him his job and eventually his freedom. He rejected my offer to send him to a renowned program for anger management. He spent three months in jail for vandalism, unpaid traffic tickets, and failure to appear in court.

I begged him to go to Adult/Teen Challenge[3] for a year. It's a wonderful program that has amazing success with helping young men like Daniel. He laughed at me and said, "No way. There is no God. There is no way I will ever go to a faith-based program."

Now this. Aggravated robbery? That's prison time for sure, five to ninety-nine years! The words I was hearing from Daniel's roommate dealt a deathblow to the dreams I had clung to for my son. Now thoroughly humbled, hopeless, buried in shame, and feeling like an utter failure as a parent, I was resigned that there was nothing more I could do for him. I told the roommate I was done. I wanted nothing more to do with this or with Daniel. For fourteen days, I refused his calls from jail. I was done. I was empty. I was defeated.

Somehow, on the fifteenth day, grace appeared, and I started breathing again. I went to see Daniel in the Dallas County jail. My body shook with a mix of anger, shame, and a mustard seed of hope that perhaps this was not over for him. Perhaps there was still a possibility of redemption, of restoration. He was still alive.

A WORD ABOUT COMPARATIVE SUFFERING . . .

Most people suffer at some point in their lives. Many endure unimaginable suffering far worse than mine or Daniel's. I cannot imagine the suffering of Dylan Roof's mom, or of the mothers of Adam Lanza, Dylan Klebold, or Eric Harris, all young men who in their pain became school shooters and then ended their own lives. I can't imagine the millions of atrocities suffered by those in the Holocaust. Who am I to tell my story of a troubled son?

We all have a story. It is in embracing your own *full* story that you find healing. Comparing your suffering to another's does you no good. Being silent about your own suffering, denying your own story because you think it is unworthy of attention compared to others, deprives you and the world of the wisdom gained by your unique experience. Marcel Proust says it well: "We are healed of a suffering only by expressing it to the full."[4] Carl Jung is even more blunt: "The foundation of mental illness *[may be]* the unwillingness to experience legitimate suffering."[5]

I can only tell my own story, my own experience. In some small way, my hope is that my wounds, although not as severe as some, will contribute to wisdom, deepen into compassion, and birth courage where there once was shame.

I believe in all that has never yet been spoken.
I want to free what waits within me
so that what no one has dared to wish for
may for once spring clear
without my contriving.
If this is arrogant, God, forgive me,
but this is what I need to say.
May what I do flow from me like a river,
no forcing and no holding back,
the way it is with children.
Then in these swelling and ebbing currents,
These deepening tides moving out, returning,
I will sing you as no one ever has,
Streaming through widening channels
into the open sea.

~ Rainer Marie Rilke[6]

THE POWER OF STORY

Story connects us. It's a human thing. We are wired for connection, and listening to others tell their stories can help us realize we are not alone. Telling your story to a trusted confidant opens the possibility for life transformation. Story helps us find meaning; it somehow touches us. The words touch our emotions and challenge our way of thinking. Knowledge, awareness, understanding, and wisdom do not come just from having someone else see your pain. It certainly helps if they are compassionate and capable of genuine empathy, but true insight and understanding will come from you feeling your pain, facing your failures, and owning your story—the real story, the one that is true and raw. This includes the ones where you were complicit in causing your own suffering, or the times you caused the suffering of another, or even those where you were an innocent victim. It is a hard thing to do, to face the truth of who you are, what you have done, or what has been done to you. But it is essential to face it, lean into it, tell it, feel it, and not run from it. So many people numb their pain by denying it, or drowning it with perfectionism, blame, or rage, or taking on their identity as a victim.

I remember my neighbor Sandra, who never let go of blame nor her identity as a victim. After ten years of marriage and two small children, Sandra's husband left her for another woman. She was devastated. I sat at her kitchen table while she screamed and yelled about the unfaithfulness of her ex-husband. She was so angry! Bitterness spewed from her mouth and flashed from her eyes. She left no space for me to say anything. She barely took a breath, just long enough to continue her tirade. I eventually moved away from the neighborhood. Twenty years later, now in our fifties, I stopped by to visit Sandra. I was astounded that she was still angry, still bitter, still blaming her ex-husband for her unhappy life, and still saying the very same sentences with the same level of bitterness she had twenty years ago! She appeared much older than her age, and her children wanted nothing to do with her; they had not come by to see her in over ten years. It is very difficult to be around an angry, bitter person who is unwilling to forgive, heal, and go on with life. A few years later, I heard that she died alone. She never remarried. She never forgave. Her heart finally quit.

So simply telling the facts of your story is not necessarily helpful; in fact, it can be damaging if the story stops at the facts. Freedom comes from telling the whole story, then recognizing our emotions related to the facts, and getting curious about how they are driving our thoughts and behaviors. With that awareness, then, change is possible. Healing is possible. Growth is possible. Peace will not come fully from having someone else just see our pain. Peace comes from telling the full story, feeling the pain, owning our part, and moving forward through forgiveness and self-compassion.

One of the first letters Daniel wrote to me from jail reminded me of Sandra's story. He was angry and blaming others, the same behaviors that resulted in his incarceration. They are the same behaviors that keep all of us bound. I knew blaming others would keep him stuck. Blame shuts the door on personal freedom. I sat down and wrote a letter back to him.

BLAME WILL KEEP YOU STUCK

Dear Daniel,

Do not get stuck blaming others. Broken people do stupid stuff. Hurt people hurt others. Let go of blame. You cannot move forward and hold on to past hurts. God knows every time your heart has been broken. He loves us unconditionally and desires to heal the brokenness and replace it with a courageous, loving, forgiving, wise heart.

You are still young and have an extraordinary future ahead of you. Choose wisely. Be courageous. Change is essential. Step into the unknown and trust that God's got you. To have a different outcome, you must be willing to do life very differently.

Your dad's greatest fear has always been abandonment, but his anger, blame, and selfishness caused the very thing he feared most. It became impossible to be around him. Fear brings torment, but perfect love casts out fear. Feel it. Forgive it. Move on. Do not hang on to an offense.

I am encouraged after talking to your lawyer. She said you might have the opportunity to request probation and twelve months at the residential treatment center, Adult/Teen Challenge in Azle, Texas. I will include the information I have on Adult/Teen Challenge at the end of this letter. Read it thoroughly and share it with your attorney. I really believe this is your best option for getting your life on track. It is time to renew your mind, cut to the root of your anger, anxiety, and impulsiveness, and become the man you were created to be—successful, peaceful, and strong, a good father, and an awesome partner to your future wife. You must be all in, commit to it, and never quit. Half-hearted and double-minded men end up living pitiful lives, leaving destruction behind them along the way.

God has a plan for your life, a plan for a future and a hope. Do not harden your heart to this opportunity. Set before you is a massive choice—an abundant life of joy and peace knowing who you are, or a life of pain, struggle, darkness, and confusion—not knowing who you are—and causing heartbreak for yourself, your precious daughter Cora, me, and everybody else who loves you. Choose life. Humble yourself and be teachable. Be hungry for the truth. It is the power of the Holy Spirit within you that renews your mind and gives you the power and wisdom to live the life you were born to live. You do not have to do all this in your own strength. You can't. I love this section of a stanza from a poem by Ted Loder, from his book *Guerillas of Grace*.[7]

"O God, gather me to be with you as you are with me. Keep me in touch with myself, with my needs, my anxieties, my angers, my pains, my corruptions, that I may claim them as my own rather than blame them on someone else."

Daniel, God does some of His best work in prison cells. It forces us to come to the end of ourselves, to be quiet long enough to hear Him and receive His transforming love. This is not religion. Religion is just another way to keep people bound. This is a personal relationship with the person of Jesus and the person of the Holy Spirit. Ask Him to fill you with His Spirit. "You will receive power when the Holy Spirit comes upon you."(Acts 1:8 NLT) You'll know.

Know that you are deeply loved. I am excited about your future. You will discover gifts and talents that you didn't even know you had. God will take you places you never dreamed of. You are blessed, gifted, a masterpiece, one of a kind, beautiful, strong, peaceful, smart, and in a position to get on the right path that will lead you to greater love, greater peace, greater prosperity, greater honor, and greater service to others. Know that you are deeply loved by all your family, including

Aunt Sue, Uncle Marty, all your cousins, and grandparents. We are all here cheering you on, believing for your salvation, redemption, restoration, and awesome future! God will cause all this to work for your good. *Mom*

THE HAPPINESS CLASS

I teach a psychology of adjustment class we call "The Happiness Course." Limited to sixteen students, the setting allows everyone the opportunity to tell his or her story. It is all by invitation. No one is ever forced to share. Through story, we examine the thoughts and feelings that drive our behavior. Some students have no problem sharing their stories; in fact, often I have to keep them from oversharing. Others though, like Anna, go the entire semester saying very little. Her demeanor was that of a tough street kid. The college is in a low-income area and most of our students are first generation college students; gangs are prevalent, and for many, English is not their first language. By the tenth week of a fifteen-week semester, trust was very high among the group. They had embraced the touchstones for the class. The touchstones are ideas that increase the likelihood of creating a safe space for individual work in community. The touchstones we used were those I learned from my formation work with the Center for Renewal and Wholeness in Education[8]. Parker Palmer describes formation as a journeying, individually and in community, to our inner selves, our hearts and souls, to identify our true selves and our deep integrity.

TOUCHSTONES [9]

1. **Be 100% present, extending and presuming welcome.** Set aside the usual distractions of things undone from yesterday, things to do tomorrow. Bring all of yourself to the work. We all learn most effectively in spaces that welcome us. Welcome others to this place and this work and presume that you are welcomed as well.

2. **Listen deeply.** Listen intently to what is said; listen to the feelings beneath the words. As Quaker writer Douglas Steere puts it, "Holy listening—to 'listen' another's soul into life, into a condition of disclosure and discovery—may be almost the greatest service that any human being ever performs for another." Listen to yourself as well as to others. Strive to achieve a balance between listening and reflecting, speaking and acting.

3. **It is never "share or die."** You will be invited to share in pairs, small groups, and in the large group. The invitation is exactly that. You will determine the extent to which you want to participate in our discussions and activities.

4. **No fixing.** Each of us is here to discover our own truths, to listen to our own inner teacher, to take our own inner journey. We are not here to set someone else straight or to help right another's wrong, to "fix" what we perceive as broken in another member of the group.

5. **Suspend judgment.** Set aside your judgments. By creating a space between judgments and reactions, we can listen to the other, and to ourselves, more fully.

6. **Identify assumptions.** Our assumptions are usually invisible to us, yet they undergird our worldview. By identifying our assumptions, we can then set them aside and open our viewpoints to greater possibilities.

7. **Speak your truth.** You are invited to say what is in your heart, trusting that your voice will be heard, and your contribution respected. Your truth may be different from, even the opposite of, what another person in the circle has said. Yet speaking your truth is simply that—it is not debating with, or correcting, or interpreting what another has said. Own your truth by remembering to speak only for yourself. Using the first person "I" rather than "you" or "everyone" clearly communicates the personal nature of your expression.

8. **Respect silence.** Silence is a rare gift in our busy world. After someone has spoken, take time to reflect without immediately filling the space with words. This applies to the speaker as well; be comfortable leaving your words to resound in the silence, without refining or elaborating on what you have just said. This process allows others time to fully listen before reflecting on their own reactions.

9. **Maintain confidentiality.** Create a safe space by respecting the confidential nature and content of discussions held in the formation circle. Allow what is said in the circle to remain there.

10. **When things get difficult, turn to wonder.** If you find yourself disagreeing with another, becoming judgmental, or shutting down in defense, try turning to wonder: "I wonder what brought her to this place?" "I wonder what my reaction teaches me?" "I wonder what he's feeling right now?

11. **Practice slowing down.** As Thomas Merton and others have cautioned, the pace of modern life can cause violent damage to the soul. By intentionally practicing slowing down, we strengthen our ability to extend non-violence to others-and to ourselves.

Late in the semester, during a paired conversation activity, I asked Anna to pair with me. I had not been fooled by her tough exterior and knew there was deep pain beneath her bravado. Within seconds of sitting down together, she began to cry and to tell me that she had considered committing suicide every day all semester. She told me a heartbreaking story of abuse at home and humiliation on the streets. In her words, "I've seen things no one my age should have to see." Something broke. She searched my eyes for judgment or shock, but without me saying a single word, what she saw was compassion and empathy born out of my own life experience. There was a sacred sharing of common pain. Anna agreed to meet with the college psychologist. Four weeks later, when final projects were due, Anna spoke up. She explained to her classmates why she had been silent and stoic for the entire semester. Her classmates listened intently with patience and respect. Anna wrote a beautiful poem she read aloud that eloquently described the labels that no longer applied to her: loser, trash, stupid, ugly, crazy, bad girl, mean. She drew us in by her awakening to new labels: beautiful, worthy, smart, resilient, strong, and brave. Her courage to do something she had never done before—tell her story—was a beautiful moment for everyone in the class. Her courage gave them courage. I keep in touch with Anna and she is thriving. The tough exterior has been replaced by a quiet confidence. She has continued with counseling and now volunteers mentoring young kids in her neighborhood. Her smile lights up the room now and she is clear that she has a purpose. She is pursuing a degree in social work. Her suffering has turned into a call. That is the power of story.

CHAPTER
2

GRASPING FOR HOPE

Dear friends, my heart is heavy today, weary to the bone. I'm heartbroken, but my hope is in God.

W hat do you do when despair overtakes you? What do you do when it appears all hope is gone? What do you do when you cannot see the next step? You are bone weary.

Dear friends,

The prosecutor said she does not want to agree to probation and will ask for the minimum five-year sentence. Daniel's attorney will call an advocate for Adult/Teen Challenge to the stand. I probably will be called to the stand as well. The prosecutor is young. I am hoping beyond hope for mercy from the judge. I'm discouraged, but I know God has Daniel in the palm of His hand. This news is a bit of a gut punch, and I'm scared. Pray I will be able to speak well on the stand and not be overcome with emotion. *Deb*

THE MIND IS A BATTLEFIELD

My Dear Daniel,

I was reminded this morning that the mind is a battlefield. I usually wake up hopeful, peaceful, and grateful. Today, however, my thoughts were dark. A cloud of shame kept whispering accusing thoughts in my head. I was caught in a whirlwind of thoughts that questioned my teaching ability, my writing, my mothering, even the intent of my heart. Thoughts of defeat, shame, and abandonment dominated.

By the front door of our house is a duffle bag with all the things you will need to go to Adult/Teen Challenge. By faith, I gathered everything and placed it there weeks ago, waiting for the word we hope for from the judge. This morning the intrusive thoughts, mocking me almost audibly, condemned me, saying, *"Daniel is not going to need those things. He's not going to make it! You might as well take them all back. You are a fool for believing he will change!"*

I know from experience that the antidote to such attack is Truth: replace the lie with the truth. Stumbling out to the backyard, I could barely breathe for the elephant on my chest. Through tears, I let out a long, sustained wail of grief. Then I shook my fist in the air, and these words erupted from deep in my innermost being: "Satan, you cannot have my boy! He belongs to God! Get your hands off him! He was dedicated to God since before he was born! Daniel is a man like Enoch who pleases God! He is a man of peace! He is a peacemaker!" The resolute authority expressed in those words both pleased me and frightened me. For twenty minutes or so, even though at that moment I did not believe what I was saying, even though it was a struggle, I paced and said aloud, "I am fearfully and wonderfully made. God is for me. There is peace in His presence. Daniel will be rescued and become all that God created him to be. God causes all things to work together for good—even our failures. My hope is in God. Come, Holy Spirit, control my thoughts. May my thoughts be in line with Your truth. May all I think, do, and say today be pleasing to You. There is now, therefore, no condemnation for those who are in Christ. He has set us free from condemnation."

Then I went into my prayer room, the quiet place where I go to get out of my head and into my heart. Still dazed and confused, I began reading Psalm 90, determined and knowing full well that the Word itself is anointed, sharper than a two-edged sword, true and powerful to get my mind, my emotions, and my spirit settled down. I wrote in my journal, "O Lord, how great is Your love for us. Your mercies are new every morning."

Then I read aloud Psalm 90:12-17: "Teach us to make the most of our time, so that we may grow in wisdom. O Lord, come back to us. How long will You delay? Take pity on Your servants! Satisfy us in the morning with Your unfailing love, so we may sing for joy to the end of our lives. Give us gladness in proportion to our former misery! Replace the evil years with good. Let us see Your miracles again; let our children see Your glory at work. And may the Lord our God show us His approval and make our efforts successful. Yes, make our efforts successful." (Ps. 90:12-17 NLT)

Then I wrote, "Lord, bless our efforts to get Daniel to Adult/Teen Challenge quickly. Restore my hope. Your word is true, and You watch over it to perform it."

By the time I finished writing, I was singing and whistling with renewed energy and hope for the day. The Word is powerful. What we choose to read, think, and say directs the course of our moments, our days, and our lives. Choose to think on good things. I learned that the words I choose to speak are more powerful than my emotions. My emotions are subject to my words. There truly is life and death in the power of the tongue.

I love verse 15: "Give us gladness in proportion to our former misery! Replace the evil years with good." We have known some misery, haven't we, Daniel? For me, the ache of betrayal, grief, and heartbreak I felt when you were angry, in a rage, cursing me, and making horrible decisions was almost too much to bear. I was so often shocked by the words that came out of your mouth, fearful of your anger, but afraid for you, too. Well . . . I am now expecting gladness in proportion to my former misery! That gladness will be great indeed!

You, too, have suffered disappointment and heartache. Now . . . expect gladness in proportion to your former misery! Confusion will be replaced with wisdom, joy for mourning, beauty for ashes, broken relationships with blessed relationships; success will replace failure, compassion and empathy will replace anger; clarity of your purpose will erase all memories of ill-fated hustling; genuine friendships will surely meet your need for love and belonging. Sonship will replace feelings of abandonment. Love, real love, true love, transforming love, will rule your heart and mind. You are blessed! Blessed means empowered to succeed.

Parker Palmer is one of my favorite authors. He wrote in *Let Your Life Speak*[10], "Vocation does not come from willfulness. It comes from listening. I must listen to my life and try to understand what it is truly about—quite apart from what I would like it to be about—or my life will never represent anything real in the world, no matter how earnest my intentions."

Raskolnikov, the character in Dostoevsky's *Crime and Punishment*[11], said "Pain and suffering are always inevitable for a large intelligence and a deep heart. The really great men must, I think, have great sadness on earth."

Daniel, when we take our brokenness, our weakness, and our fears and lay them at the feet of Jesus and say, "Lord, take my life and make something good of it. Give me wisdom to choose rightly, a spirit to receive, and faith to act; make me an honorable man that I may serve others with a pure heart. Rescue me. Bless me beyond what I can ask or think. Keep your hand upon me that I do no harm—only good" then . . .hang on . . . God will move heaven and earth to rescue you, provide for you, and take you places you never dreamed!

I love you forever and always,

Expectant and hopeful,

Wholeheartedly for you,

Mom

That letter describes a time when somehow, although quite messy and undignified, I was finally able to get a handle on my emotions and speak truth. There were many times when I needed someone to come alongside. My sister Susan would pray when I couldn't pray. She took care of Daniel when I could not get off the couch. Lifelong friends Bill and Jane would take my desperate calls in the middle of the night. There indeed is beauty for ashes. Weeping may last for a night, but joy comes in the morning. Not always the very next morning—but joy does come. If we could just remember that suffering is temporary when we are in the middle of the mess! Pain deceives us into thinking it will always be this way. The truth is that what is seen is subject to change. May we cry out for grace to sustain us when our strength is gone.

STRUGGLING TO MAKE SENSE OF THE MESS

The despair Daniel felt while in jail was evident in his second letter to me. He, too, felt defeat, shame, and abandonment. Since he was not yet equipped with a skill set to deal with despair, his letter is a mix of regret and doubt, grasping for a glimmer of hope.

Mom,

Today, I let the stress and anxiety of being helpless in here really get the best of me. I am very sorry for that and for taking it out on you over the phone. It is really the first day since I have been here that I felt I just wanted to break down, and I felt miserable about the situation that I put myself in. You are right that it is all my own fault and stupidity that put me here. I brought this all on myself. I dug myself this hole, and now I have to lay in it. Whenever I start thinking about losing my baby daughter Cora, or not seeing her at this time in her life, that is when all my walls break down, and I just feel alone. Being in jail makes it so much worse. I do not have anyone to talk to, so I am sorry I took it out on you today. I love you. I don't know if you will ever really understand how alone I really am. I don't have anyone else that answers the phone like you do. My dad has not answered since the first time I called him. My two "friends" won't pick up the phone, and they stole all my money and belongings.

This letter isn't supposed to make you, or anyone, feel bad; I just want you to understand where my head is at . . . the stress of my situation is really getting to me and I feel like everyone is just moving on without me. I feel like I have to put this on paper or I'll never feel any better. It seems like the past four years of my life, the only "adult" years of my life, have been absolutely nothing but a mess. And it is all my fault. It really started when I lost my family. Morgen and I never really treated each other right, ever. Both of us always did something to ruin the trust or hurt each other, and we really weren't even ready for what we threw ourselves into. I began to drink too much, and she did too. That only led to more arguing and more doing things to hurt each other. By the time Cora was three, we had no respect for each other, and even though we tried, we both knew there were too many cracks in the picture to fix it. It was going to shatter eventually. I knew I had lost Morgen and any hope I had of Cora growing up in a sound, intact family way before I had actually lost them and moved out. I just stopped caring about Morgen, about my work, our home life, even my personal life. I just didn't care anymore. I don't think I ever "fixed" that broken part inside me. I stopped working as hard as I was. I was distracted, and I knew my boss noticed. Then when he fired me, I couldn't keep a job at any other print shops either. I even stopped caring about my probation, and it got me in even more trouble. I was putting my own self-medicating ways before my family, among other things, just like my dad did and I lost them, just like my dad did.

When Morgen and I started to have problems, we told each other we didn't want Cora to grow up in a broken family like we both did, but it wasn't enough. We both gave up early. But now, I'm finally realizing that I let her and that whole situation completely take a choke hold on my life. I lost control of myself, my priorities, lost sight of my goals, and began to drink even more and self-medicate even more. Even after I moved and "started over," I was still depressed that I caused my family to be broken and it's still messing with me to this day.

Still, my own self-guilt and anger are causing me to make decisions I would never, ever, ever choose to do out of my own free will. If I wasn't completely blacked out on Xanax and alcohol, I would have never made the mistake that ended me up in jail right now. Never. I know that doesn't justify anything or make it any better, but it's true. I never do illegal things like that. I don't hang around people who do, and I usually don't even think like that. I truly don't know what I was thinking that day. All I know now is that this is more than enough of a wake-up call than I'll ever need to do right for the rest of my entire life. It's more than enough of a scare to make me realize that I want to be there for you when you need me, and for Cora when she needs me and while she is growing up. That little girl means more to me than anything else. You know that, mom. I can't go to prison and miss out on everything just because of some stupid, dumb decision I made when I wasn't thinking clearly. I recognize my potential. I know I'm better than that and the choices I've made in the past three or four years.

I love you. I love Cora. I love my own life way too much to let this and my habits ruin the future I envisioned for myself and my family. You and Cora are all that matter to me. Family is all I have. I don't have any friends. I don't have anything that belongs to me: no money, no cars, no reputation, nothing.

I can't act like I'm not scared because I am. I'm terrified. Anything can happen on the 29th of this month. Whatever judgment they give me, I'll have to take it because it's what God said that I deserve. I pray every day and every night before I sleep that He gives me this "second chance." I will take it and run. Everyone will be able to see a visible difference in my morals and decision-making. The most important thing to me is not losing my family again.

Again, I'm sorry I was so stressed out on the phone and rude towards you. I love you more than anything, Mom. You are literally all that I've got. Please, don't give up on me now.

I always think about the small things, like being able to clean your pool out for you. I didn't really enjoy the chore when I was free, but man, I sure would love to do it right now, or any other small chore you had for me. I would love it.

I do not want to go to prison. I know what I've done could quite possibly send me there and it's a scary thought. I don't want to miss out on anything. I don't want a family member to pass away or for Cora to miss me one more single day then she has to. I'm putting all my faith in God and praying as hard as I can that He gives me this second chance. I know if He does, I'll never mess up again. I never want to spend another night in one of these cells, and I can't imagine having to spend years or even many months like this. I know it wouldn't even shape my behavior. I have realized what I needed to realize and that's that my life is so valuable.

Thank you incredibly much for sending me books and putting money on the phones and commissary. I don't do jail well. Some people can, I can't. Another reason I know I don't belong here or prison. I'm better than this place and you raised me better. I love you. I know one day soon I will make you so proud . . . I know it.

It is about 3:00 AM right now. I slept all day, so I can't sleep. I've written Morgen and Cora a long letter, but I think God just wanted me to write it to get some things off my chest. I don't think it's meant to be read by anyone. Thank you for showing me God. Thank you for showing me peace, forgiveness, love, patience, and most of all right now, how to humble myself. Thank you for raising me the right way even when it would have been easier to let me run myself into a wall. I love you so much, Mom. You are my best friend.

Daniel

BECOMING AWARE—THE FIRST STEP TOWARD THE PATH OF WISDOM

This letter is quite sad, but it also shows that Daniel is becoming aware. It is the first faltering step toward wisdom for living. The hardness and rage are gone. He is attempting to identify what he is feeling and is struggling to make sense of the events that led him to do the things that put him in jail. These initial signs of becoming aware will grow into greater insight if he presses on and refuses to shrink back into self-pity or blaming others. This is the messy middle. Life crashed. There was a loss of freedom, a loss of control, a loss of love and of belonging. This stage of becoming aware is very painful and nearly always chaotic and confusing—the messy middle. Many folks give up in this stage. The messy middle is hard. It is easier to blame others or wallow in self-pity and never move beyond that. However, for wisdom to grow, it is essential to stay in the messy middle and keep on being curious. Choose to believe that there is a way out of the chaos. Even though you may not see how yet, there is a way and it will become clear. You will discover the next right thing to do.

The struggle is real. We struggle with identity: who am I? Is there any hope for change? We struggle with our thoughts and our words. We struggle with our emotions, with setting healthy boundaries, and we certainly struggle with hope and faith. It is helpful to get used to the idea of struggle. Choosing "easy" is rarely the best course of action. Struggling produces endurance. Endurance produces character. Failing to lean in to the struggle will cause us automatically to revert to the default ways that have not worked in the past, this time with even more devastating consequences.

Becoming aware, the first step on the journey toward wisdom, on the quest for wholeness, is especially grueling because we may not yet have a skill set to navigate the hard things. This book is an attempt to give you that skill set. As you keep reading, keep hoping, keep doing the next right thing, you are building a strong foundation for a life well lived. Pursue wisdom. It will not accidentally land on your head. You choose first to desire wisdom for living; then you pursue it. Read. Look for others with more insight than you currently have and talk to them. Find a mentor. Pray. Do whatever you can to eliminate those things contrary to wisdom. That may mean severing toxic relationships or turning off the television. Fix your mind on your desire for wisdom for living. Many people desire to run a marathon, but they never get off the couch, put on running shoes, and walk the first one hundred yards. What can you do right now to put yourself in the best position possible to learn wisdom? What resources are available to you right now?

It is a difficult thing to want to change. Dallas Willard, in his book, *Renovation of the Heart*[12], describes how change occurs—not only spiritual transformation, but any change. He uses the acronym VIM, which stands for vision, intention, means. We first must have a vision for a better way to be. Then, we set our intention, which involves choice. Finally, we search for and put in place the means for learning a new way of being. How sad that so many people never get a glimpse or a hope of a better way to be! For them to passively accept their lot in life is quite tragic. I believe as teachers, parents, and friends, it is our responsibility to encourage the despondent by painting pictures of a life of hope and of a path out of the chaos, and by proposing specific "means"—that is, tools, books, examples, mentoring—that can help them find that better path.

CHAPTER
3

IDENTITY

Teach me who I am

Daniel struggled with his identity as most of us do. There was a huge gap between how I saw him and how he saw himself. I wish I could tell you I was always gracious and helpful when writing to Daniel, but this particular day I was angry. This letter shows my struggle, and it challenges Daniel's view of himself.

CHALLENGING HOW YOU SEE YOURSELF

Daniel,

Your attitude has everything to do with your future. If you continue to think that you are a victim, that future will not be good. Take responsibility for what you have done. Humble yourself and admit your thinking was all wrong. Desire above all things to renew your mind. Learn to think in healthy, hopeful ways rather than arrogant, self-serving ways.

It is obvious that your thinking has been way wrong. It never crosses the mind of a healthy, humble person to rob a store. A healthy, humble person does not use drugs or steal or pick a fight at the drop of a hat. A healthy, humble person does not say vile, hurtful things to others. A healthy, humble, grateful person does not throw a fit or explode in rage when he doesn't get his way. A healthy, humble person is encouraging and grateful. A messed-up narcissist criticizes others and justifies his hurtful behavior.

According to our phone conversation yesterday, you were mad because you think Morgen is keeping Cora from you. The truth is, your actions, your felony, your drug use disqualify you from the right to be around a child. The only way you will ever get to be in Cora's life is to change. Blaming others will keep you locked in self-pity, rage, and destructive behavior. Accepting, admitting, and feeling remorse over your own actions will open the door for God to bring correction, restoration, and the wisdom to think, feel, and act with civility.

You also implied that you think somehow you do not deserve punishment. There are real and severe consequences for breaking the law. You blame the system. Really? There has to be a system to protect society from people who think they do not have to obey the law.

It baffles me to try and make sense of why you see yourself as a victim, a rebel, a low-life criminal, when the truth is you were given everything you needed to construct a successful, honorable life. You didn't want to hang around with good kids. You wanted to hang around troubled, drug-using, lazy, disrespectful kids despite every effort I made to steer you in the right direction.

Well, you are an adult now. Do you still want to see yourself as a victim, a rebel, a low-life criminal? You could be graduating from college about now. You could have money in the bank, good friendships, and special relationships with your family, cousins, and me. Nobody excluded you. You excluded yourself by choosing to do just the opposite of what builds connection. I remember having you write a hundred times when you were about twelve, "I do not steal because I am honest. I do not use drugs because I am smarter than that. I am respectful and grateful for every opportunity given to me."

I cannot express strongly enough the immense importance of the decision before you now. It is life or death. You can humble yourself, kneel broken before God, and ask Him to teach you, save you, renew your mind, order your steps, fix what is broken in you, take your life and do something good with it. Or you can continue to manipulate, blame, be angry, lack self-control, be pitiful, and rationalize your arrogance and rebellion to look cool to the other low-lifes and live a life that is getting more and more destructive.

Set before you are life and death. Choose life. Choose to surrender all to God who loves you and stands ready to put the broken pieces back together to make a beautiful tapestry of your life; to give you a life you never dreamed of; to take you places you never imagined; to place you in a family that you can serve motivated only by love.

God causes all things to work together for good for those who love Him. The key is "to those who love him." You cannot continue to cling to this imposter self you have created and want things your way and expect God to work all things together for your good. Your own way will continue to cause chaos, heartbreak, and severe consequences.

Go to church right there in jail. You probably don't want to go because you won't look cool. Lay down your stupid pride. You are trying to impress the wrong people. If you make a move to seek God, He will run to you.

Pray this:

"Forgive me. Please forgive me because I have been rebellious, arrogant, angry, and have gone my own way. Forgive me for the hurtful words I've spoken to others. Forgive me for rejecting You, Your love, and Your way. Forgive me for cursing You, for cursing my mother, for blaming my father, for blaming Morgen. Forgive me for stealing. Forgive me for scaring the man at the store. Forgive me for dishonoring my mom. Forgive me for the heartache I have caused. Forgive me for the shame I have brought on my family. Take my life and do something good with it because I sure have messed it up. Teach me to follow You, to love You with my whole heart, all my mind, and all my strength. Lead me. Teach me. Humble me that I may learn Your ways and love Your law. I accept the consequences I deserve. I ask You for mercy. Put me in a place for me to be taught, mentored, and ministered to so that I can know who I am in You. Make me teachable. I ask You to allow me to go to Adult/Teen Challenge for twelve months. With Your help, God, I will commit myself, submit myself to those in authority over me, and set my mind and heart to be transformed into the man You created me to be. Your will be done, Lord. Not mine."

It is too hurtful to me to talk to you while you are still blaming, controlling, angry, and selfish. You do not even realize how distorted your thinking is. You do not even realize how hurtful your words and actions are.

Begin now, even before Adult/Teen Challenge, to renew your mind. Read the Bible. Pray with humility and total dependence on God. Live every day, starting today, with a burning desire to change—to allow God to change you. Read the Word of God and do what it says. Be grateful—sincerely thankful for everything.

Your words have power. Life and death are in the power of the tongue. Speak life. Stop criticizing your attorney and be grateful for her. Pray for her to have wisdom and favor. Stop being afraid of the judge; instead, pray for her to have wisdom and mercy.

Forgive everybody for everything. Forgive your dad. Forgive Morgen. Forgive me. Remaining bitter and unforgiving will keep you locked in a prison even after you are let out. Sincere forgiveness will set your spirit free. Do not harden your heart. Be kind, gentle, patient, loving, faithful, forgiving, peaceful, trusting, and humble.

Mom

DARE TO LISTEN

I was asked to do a TEDx talk in 2015 about daring. I wanted to share a bit of my story in my message and when it came to talking about Daniel, who at the time was still angry, rebellious, and involved in very risky behavior, I decided to "call things that are not as though they were." I still believed that Daniel would turn his life around some day and I didn't want this TEDx talk, which would be in perpetuity on the internet, to expose the dark period in his life. I was not lying when in the talk I said, "Daniel is a fine, wonderful young man." I was indeed speaking in faith and calling things that are not as though they already were.

TEDX TALK [13]

When we dare to listen, amazing things happen. "I want to hear your story. Who are you? What do you dream of? What do you desire? What brings you joy?" I'll never forget the moment a dear friend asked me those questions and sincerely and compassionately listened to me. All too often when I ask people these questions, they don't know how to answer; perhaps they have forgotten. I know there have been times when I struggled to answer these for myself. We become disconnected or "dis-integrated" from what we once knew. Instead of connecting with our past, we unknowingly create imposter selves motivated by fear rather than faith. Here is what I know: fear brings torment, but faith is the foundation—the building block for our hopes and dreams, the substance of things hoped for.

We need a shift in our thinking that reminds each of us who we are at our highest, best, and most sacred selves. Then we can have faith for what we can accomplish together, when we each are a bit more integrated, whole, and living from a place of integrity. I think this may be what Thomas Merton[14] called the true self. Quakers call it the inner teacher. It is an abiding selfhood—the soul, or spirit of a person.

The disconnection or dis-integration is a 'divided life.' Living divided represents 'the disconnect' between who we are and what we do—between our soul and our role.[15] A divided life may look like this:

1. We don't enjoy our work, and it disconnects us from those we are meant to serve.
2. We stay in relationships that kill our spirit and violate our values.
3. We become "people pleasers" or become arrogant and angry.
4. We hide our true identities out of fear of being criticized or rejected.
5. Without our being aware of it, we take on an "imposter self.[16]"

I think learning to listen to others in life-giving ways first requires us to learn or re-learn to listen to ourselves. Listen to that still, small voice that you recognize as your own, that affirms who you are and reveals the purpose and meaning for your life. Here are five questions: "Who am I? What do I love? What do I believe? What is my gift? How then shall I live?[17] The first question is, "Who am I?" If I am not sure who I am, I become way too vulnerable to projections others place on me. I unconsciously armor up and try to fit into what's expected of me, making life a struggle rather than a flow. It's like trying to wear a coat that is three sizes too small. You may squeeze yourself into it, but it distorts your thinking, causing you to live small.

There was a period of my life where I was lost. In hindsight, I clearly was dis-integrated for several years. There is a huge chasm between who I am now and what my life looked like during that time. After a successful teaching career loving my work, my home, my friends, and my life, at age 39 I married who I thought was the love of my life. The first six weeks were the happiest I had ever been. I loved my life. I loved my husband. Daniel was conceived right away, and life was good!

The seventh week began a downward spiral toward despair, a systematic unraveling of everything I believed. My faith, hope, and love were shattered by violence and betrayal. I spent the next several years trying to remember who I was. It was shame that dis-integrated my sense of self, shame for getting into this mess and shame for not knowing how to get out. My confidence was destroyed. I clearly was in a state of dis-integration, and it was fear that kept me in that broken state.

We all have a story. Perhaps your challenge came in a different form than mine, but the outcome is probably somewhat similar: varying degrees of dis-integration. Dis-integration can be imposed by a toxic relationship, as in my case, or imposed by a whole culture that inflicts limitations by dehumanizing others through anger, shame, blame, racism, sexism, or ageism. Most damaging of all is the inner critic—the voice that lies to us saying, "I am not enough. I am somehow hopelessly flawed." When we allow this voice in, we think small and we live small. If you wear the restricting coat, the emotional armor, long enough, it disconnects you from your true self— the you that had noble dreams, the you that knew what brought you joy, knew what you wanted and absolutely believed was possible, and the you that laughed easily and loved life.

I struggled with many questions, growing more frustrated with each passing year that I couldn't figure out the answers. "What is it about me that allowed this to happen? Where do I belong? What am I supposed to do? What is my purpose?" These are not inherently bad questions, but the answers were unattainable without the bedrock Truth on which a life is built. These questions are all about the "doing" rather than the "being" of life. The answers we seek may not be in those "doing" questions at all but in affirmative true declarations of "being." I am. I am enough. I am worthy. There are a lot of ways I am not broken, but deeply and profoundly whole. You are. You are enough. You are worthy. You belong. You are loved.[4] Now, knowing what to do, knowing my purpose, and discerning my gift to humankind comes more easily because it flows out of who I am.

I am a teacher. Teachers are trained to prepare for "what" we will teach, "how" we will teach it, and if we go deeper, "why" we teach it, but as Parker Palmer says, we rarely ask, "who"—who is the teacher who teaches?

You fill in the blank, "I am a—leader, CEO, mom, dad, student," whatever your role. To some degree, you were trained for what you do, how to do it, and maybe even why you do it. Ask the "who" question. Who is the leader who leads? Who is the student who learns? Who is the CEO who guides the organization?

At times, the "who," (the me) that was trying to teach was functioning out of ego or fear. I can tell you that when we are

driven by ego or fear, it rarely turns out well. I was overly sensitive to criticism. I thought I needed recognition and affirmation. I was hustling for worthiness, and it was exhausting!
All of these are fear-based thoughts, emotions, and behaviors.
Fear of failure, fear of not being good enough, manifested in
self-doubt and sometimes, I'm ashamed to say it, manifested
in blaming others. That's what fear does. Connection to your
true self gets you out of fear and into wholeness, into "being"
rather than "doing," into courage and compassion.

When I parented my son, Daniel, out of fear rather than
love, the result was not good. Fear can look like judgment
and feel like rejection to a child, and to anybody for that
matter. I finally figured out that my job was not to fix him
but to love him. My job was to nurture the gifts I saw in him.
My son, Daniel, is now twenty and is a kind, gentle, and amazing young man. He still catches me trying to make everything
a teachable moment, and he gently reminds me how frustrat-
ing that is to him, assuring me I did a good job and that he is
alright.

Ego and fear cause disconnection, and learning, leading,
and parenting are all about connections. Whatever our work
is, when we try to operate with intellect alone we fall short.
We fail to make those vital connections with others. We wear
our busyness like a badge. Doing too much too fast does not
allow time or presence for connections.

We all have a story. So many of us struggle and strain to
find the words to tell our story with our whole heart. We may
not even know our story anymore because we have become
dis-integrated and disconnected. Maybe we have not found

safe spaces to tell our story. Maybe we are listening to fear rather than courage, rendering us victims rather than community builders, causing us to isolate rather than connect, to lash out rather than embrace. Dr. Martin Luther King, Jr. said many times, "Violence is the language of the unheard."[18]

When we have been heard, things begin to make sense. I have deeply appreciated the times that I have experienced sensitive, empathic, and concentrated listening.[19] I also deeply appreciate the times when I've been given the honor of listening to another and witnessing their re-integration when they remember whom they are, what they love, what they believe, and what brings them joy.

What if we listened to that voice in all of us that loves justice and mercy? What if each of us functioned from a belief in our own worthiness? What if we believed we could co-create a world of non-violence? What if we believed we could create a more civil society?

When we ask the right questions, when we listen deeply to one another without judgment, when we recognize our common humanity, when we take off the armor and allow ourselves to be seen, when we are willing to identify the broken places in our hearts and invite healing and freedom, vulnerability and courage—then, and only then, can we live wholeheartedly. Then, and only then, can we walk the walk that invites others to live wholeheartedly, too.

When we respect the wisdom and experience in each other, a climate is created in which people are empowered, no longer victims of circumstance but co-creators of a new reality.

Let's create a culture where we invite everyone's voice to be heard. Let's invite courage, compassion, and connection in our classrooms, in our board rooms, in our organizations, in our communities, and in our families. Let's take the time to create safe spaces to listen and to speak our own truth.

When what we do flows out of who we are at our best, most authentic, highest selves, then our work is meaningful. We listen to courage rather than fear. We build connections and become more compassionate with ourselves and with each other.

Life is good. Life is really good when we dare to listen to ourselves and hear who we are and what we love, when we recognize our gift to others, and when we allow our doing to flow out of our being, out of our more integrated, true self. When we dare to listen, amazing things happen.

You can watch this presentation for yourself at *https://www.youtube.com/watch?v=Dfpj33DGk4o&t=35s*

TRANSFORMATION OF THE HEART

Dear Daniel,

Do you want a new identity? Suffering has a way of teaching us wisdom if we dare to listen. Humility has a way of leading us from shame to honor. Pride in our own ability leads to a fall, but being humbled leads to a teachable spirit that will little by little lift us out of despair and into joy.

A wise person first believes that God is, and that He is the rewarder of those who seek Him. Even though we cannot see God, we can experience His presence through deep listening. The fruit of the Spirit in us produces love, joy, peace, patience, kindness, goodness, faithfulness, gentleness, and self-control. We cannot produce this fruit, this right way of living, in our own strength. If we try to do life through intellect alone, we fall way short. It is Christ in us. It is the Holy Spirit in us, around us, and for us, that enables us to make right choices and ultimately to fulfill our calling—to do the work He predetermined us to do. He works in us to will and to do His good pleasure. We receive all of this by faith. He does all the work. Our role is to believe and receive. We pray "Fill me, Lord, with your spirit. Bless me that I may be a blessing to others." I like the way St. Paul puts it:

My counsel is this: Live freely, animated and motivated by God's Spirit. Then you won't feed the compulsions of selfishness. For there is a root of sinful self-interest in us that is at odds with a free spirit, just as the free spirit is incompatible with selfishness. These two ways of life are antithetical, so that you cannot live at times one way and at times another way according to how you feel on any given day. Why don't you choose to be led by the Spirit and so escape the erratic compulsions of a law-dominated existence?

It is obvious what kind of life develops out of trying to get your own way all the time: repetitive, loveless, cheap sex; a stinking accumulation of mental and emotional garbage; frenzied and joyless grabs for happiness; trinket gods; magic-show religion; para-noid loneliness; cutthroat competition; all-consuming-yet-never-satisfied wants; a brutal temper; an impotence to love or be loved; divided homes and divided lives;

small-minded and lopsided pursuits; the vicious habit of depersonalizing everyone into a rival; uncontrolled and uncontrollable addictions; ugly parodies of community. I could go on. This isn't the first time I have warned you, you know. If you use your freedom this way, you will not inherit God's kingdom.

But what happens when we live God's way? He brings gifts into our lives, much the same way that fruit appears in an orchard—things like affection for others, exuberance about life, serenity. We develop a willingness to stick with things, a sense of compassion in the heart, and a conviction that a basic holiness permeates things and people. We find ourselves involved in loyal commitments, not needing to force our way in life, able to marshal and direct our energies wisely.

— Galatians 5:16-24 in *The Message* (MSG)

Your heavenly Father already knows all your needs, and He will give you all you need from day to day if you live for Him and make the Kingdom of God your primary concern (Matthew 6:33 NLT). Take delight in the Lord, and He will give you your heart's desire (Psalm 37:4).

Choose to believe He loves you, is for you, and will reveal Himself to you. He will show Himself mighty on your behalf. I truly believe God has a plan for your life. He will use all your experiences, work them together for good, and you will be equipped to help many, many people avoid disaster and live lives of purpose, righteousness, peace, and joy. I am so anxious and excited to see you come into who you are. You are creative, wise, talented, compassionate, articulate, strong, humble, and courageous. It is going to be amazing to see what God does through you when you give your life to Him completely.

I pray for great favor to be upon you. I pray for mercy from the judge and that you will be able to go to Adult/Teen Challenge very soon. I pray the Spirit of God will reveal truth to you, will amplify His word to you, and will protect you, order your steps, and equip you to be all He created you to be and to do. I love you forever and always.

Mom

PART 2
BECOMING MINDFUL
Teach me to think

CHAPTER
4

THOUGHTS AND WORDS

As you think, so you are

D r. Caroline Leaf, a cognitive neuroscientist, in her book Switch on your Brain affirms this truth: "Thoughts are real, physical things that occupy mental real estate. Moment by moment, every day, you are changing the structure of your brain through your thinking. When we hope, it is an activity of the mind that changes the structure of our brain in a positive and normal direction."[20] The good news is that we can choose what we think about. You do not have to accept or dwell on every thought that comes to your mind. You can choose to reject a thought or to accept a thought. In order to retrain your brain, it is essential that you intentionally choose what to think about. At first, habitual ways of thinking may seem permanent or irreversible. However, you can learn to practice controlling your thought life. You can choose to challenge a thought by asking, *"Is this true? Does this thought line up with who I want to be?"* You can then reject or accept the thought. When I was first learning to do this, I found it extremely helpful to say my decision out loud. When I was feeling unworthy, I would say out loud, "I am worthy! I choose to believe that there is goodness in me. I reject the lie that I am unworthy." At first, it felt like I was lying to myself because my emotions were screaming at me, "You are so broken!" But I was thrilled to learn that emotions follow thoughts. Emotions don't drive me now. Taking control of my thought life is the principle driver. My emotions have no choice but to follow my thought life. In effect, it is rewiring your brain, back to what and who you are at your best, highest, most sacred self. Our lives are not simply victims of genetics and life experiences. How we choose to "think" about our life experiences is far more powerful in determining the quality of our lives.

I am sure you can now see how incredibly important it is to set healthy boundaries to prevent lies from having a free-for-all with your thought life. It becomes necessary to remove from your life people who are cynical, critical, and mean spirited. Words are like poisonous darts. Every negative word injects its poison into your soul. We need to be intentional about who we allow to speak into our lives. We cannot avoid all negativity, but I sincerely believe most people have no boundaries, thereby making themselves victims without even being aware of it. You can tell very quickly what is *life-giving* and what is *death-dealing* if you learn to pay attention to your visceral response. Over time, you become more and more sensitive to the power of words if you practice mindfulness and body awareness. If a person has been subjected to negative talk for a long time, this process may require an all-out effort.

It is that important. It is a matter of life and death. It is a matter of fulfilling your destiny or allowing others to steal your destiny. It is a matter of living wholeheartedly or living small—way below your calling.

THOUGHTS BECOME THINGS

My Dear Daniel,

It was heart breaking to see you in such discouragement yesterday. As your mom, I want to see you happy, hopeful, and at peace. I know this is a very difficult time for you. It's hard on me, too. But I know that it is temporary, and you will get past this and be stronger for it. Driving home from our visit yesterday, I declared out loud in my car, "God will lift Daniel up! There is no pit too deep that God cannot find you. He will cause all of this to work together for your good. God is close to the brokenhearted. He will give you beauty for ashes, joy for mourning. God will lift you up, Daniel!"

Your life will progress in the direction of your thoughts. What you think about comes about. Thoughts become things. That is why it is essential to choose what you think about. Whenever you begin to dwell on all the reasons life appears hopeless, you can change the direction of your thoughts. I know it seems difficult when you just saw the man in your cell there receive a life sentence when he expected a much lighter penalty. I know it is difficult to think positive thoughts when you are lonely, or ashamed, or angry, or discouraged. But the good news is that you do have power. You do have the immense power and freedom to choose what you think about.

It is all about what you choose to focus on. If your mindset is that of a victim, you will think, feel, and act like a victim. The emotions that follow that train of thought are dark and destructive. If your mindset is that of a victor, you will think, feel, and act like a victor. Despite the circumstances you are in right now, you can still choose what you focus on. To keep hope alive, you must read encouraging and hopeful words. You must choose to believe that God loves you, knows exactly where you are, and knows why you were driven to do the things that got you there. He still loves you completely and unconditionally. He will strengthen your inner man. He, the Holy Spirit, will teach you, counsel you, and comfort you. He is going before you to prepare the way for you to be completely free, restored, and blessed. He is providing the favor, the teachers, the mentors, the instruction, the insight, the understanding, the healing for past hurts, the discipline of mind, and the faith to trust Him.

Your part is to choose faith. Choose to give your life to the One who alone has the power and transforming love to arrange things in your favor. Choose to believe He will open the right doors for you, pardon your sin, and work within you to make you the extraordinary man He created you to be and equip you to do the good works He prepared for you to do even before you were born. He, the Holy Spirit, will teach you and empower you to be an extraordinary father to Cora. He will lead you to truth. He will teach you to discern the right path for your life.

Nobody can do life right on his or her own. We all fall short and live, at best, a mediocre life. At worst, we cause damage to ourselves and everybody in our lives. Apart from God, we do not even know how to love. Apart from God, we can do nothing of real lasting value. But the good news is that we can do all things through Christ who strengthens us. First, believe that He is. A fool says there is no God. But even faith as small as a mustard seed can move a mountain.

Then trust that He rewards those who seek Him. We make the slightest turn towards Him and He runs to us just as a loving father runs to his son or daughter who calls out, "Daddy, I need you. Help me."

I did not come to the end of myself until I was twenty-nine. Up until that time my life was filled with anxiety, depression, a string of broken relationships, and hustling to feel worthy. Up until then, even though Aunt Sue tried to tell me about God for years, I rejected Him. I was arrogant and said I can do life on my own. But I was empty. Something in me told me there had to be more.

When another relationship failed, I was broken, exhausted, and alone in my house; I fell to my knees and said, "God, if you are there, take my life and do something good with it because all I see is blackness." I woke up the next morning different. I call it my "awakening." I had a glimmer of hope that it was possible to learn to do life better.

My desires immediately began to change. Instead of mocking the things of God, I was drawn to learn about Him. My interests changed. I started going to church. I met new friends. I learned that I chose to get into relationships with guys for all the wrong reasons and would either sabotage a relationship with a good guy who treated me better than I thought I deserved or date a guy who treated me poorly. The latter felt more hauntingly congruent with my distorted sense of self. I have since learned that we date at the level of our own self-esteem. In fact, we choose friends at the level of our own self-esteem too. I did not see myself as worthy of better. Until we know our own value, we hang out with those who confirm our own distorted perceptions of ourselves. We are incapable of giving or receiving genuine love and belonging until we know our own worthiness.

I pursued Truth with all my might. I took a leave of absence from the college where I taught, put a "for sale" sign in my yard, and loaded up my Chevy Blazer with my bike and backpacking tent. I knew I had to find someone I trusted to teach me about life and about God. Bill and Jane Robinson came to mind immediately. Bill and Jane came into my life in 1972 at Skyline High School in Dallas, twelve years prior to my "awakening." My brother, David, was in Jane's class directly across the hall from my classroom. I was a lost, confused teenager without a clue about how to do life. Hustling for a sense of belonging was a way of being for me that was exhausting and fruitless.

I was drawn like a magnet to Jane because she accepted me as I was in all my brokenness. I skipped school more than I showed up, so Jane would check on me every morning and give me a star on the days I showed up. I couldn't care less about the star, but her caring, her noticing, her seeing me—truly seeing me—undid me. Could it be, that if this teacher cared, that I was worthy of being?

Bill was a student at Dallas Theological Seminary at that time, and both he and Jane invested time and attention to me.

They never "preached," but I knew they had something I wanted: a peace, a purpose, a genuine kindness.

I called them the morning after my "awakening." They graciously agreed to let me come to Bremerton, Washington, and stay with them for a while. I stayed three months. I picked Bill's brain. I watched Jane. I saw how they did life so well. What is this easy, genuine love I see? Still, there was no preaching, just living life and letting me live with them. They showed me the character of a man called Jesus. They demonstrated the reality of life with the Life Giver. They never dismissed me. They never rushed me. I treasure that time with them. They were pastors of Peninsula Bible Fellowship. Church was awkward for me, but still I was drawn by the feeling of acceptance—of love and belonging.

I returned to Dallas in late October of 1984 with a deep desire to continue this search for the way to live a life of joy and excellence. I decided not to date for a year while I learned about God and who I was. It turned out to be ten years. I stayed in church, I read the Bible, and I prayed for God to show me who He was, who I was, and why I was here. I did not want empty religion. I wanted Truth. Over time, I got a bit more emotionally healthy and happy. I met your father in 1994 at his parents' house. There was a week-long revival going on at the church there in Waco where Aunt Sue and Uncle Marty attended. Your father and I went to the revival every night. Your dad was baptized that week.

We got married in July of 1994. I resigned from teaching, moved to Waco, and I was the happiest I had ever been in my life. I was so excited about you. I planned on home schooling you and having a couple more kids. I was writing and teaching some in the church. Life was so beautiful. Your father was fun, and I thought he was committed to you and me. However, by the time you were three months old, he got really mean. I later discovered he was addicted to cocaine and had been leading a double life. I tried my best to get him help. The church tried. Marty and Sue tried their best to help him. And—you know the story—he got more and more violent and impossible to live with. The church helped get you and me to a safe house. I was devastated. My dreams were shattered. I began to question everything I believed about God. Why didn't God save your father, save our marriage, keep our family intact? It took years for me to recover and to finally understand that God was certainly willing and able to help your dad, but there is this thing called "free will." God gives us free will. Your dad chose to reject help. He chose drugs, pornography, infidelity, lies, and a very dark life instead of choosing us. He refused to submit himself to counseling, ministry, treatment or anything. His arrogance, pride, and selfishness destroyed our family, his business, and eventually his health. He refused to be teachable. He refused to submit himself to God, or to any person or program that could have changed the course of his life—and ours. The Bible is true when it says, "Pride goes before a fall." I imagine he thought he could manage both sides of his double life—have it all. But that is not possible. A double-minded man is unstable in all his ways. If you leave a crack for the devil, he will destroy your house.

I believe, and many psychologists believe, that what happens is that healthy development stops at the age a person starts using drugs. Your dad started using drugs in his late teens or early twenties. He never matured beyond that age. I don't know, but perhaps by the time I met him in his late thirties, he was too far gone. He had lived a lie for so long he didn't know how to be truthful. I have long since forgiven him. I wish him only good things. Free will is a powerful thing. Sometimes I wonder why God gave us free will. The paradox of God's sovereignty and free will is a mystery to me. Both are true. God is sovereign. We have free will.

Your brain is still developing. An adult's brain is not fully developed until age twenty-five. Using marijuana, alcohol, or drugs compromises healthy development. It can do permanent damage. It is foolish to think a person can mature and grow more responsible by altering brain chemistry as new neuronal connections are being made. It is idiotic and self-serving to deny the truth and believe the lie that marijuana is harmless. It's especially stupid to claim it is helpful. Do not be deceived. A fool only looks for ways to confirm his own deceptive beliefs.

I believe your family can be restored. You are only twenty-one. I believe you can learn, mature, and develop fully into the man God designed you to be. It will require admitting you have been wrong and turning another direction. Submit yourself to God, to teaching, to mentoring, and to a structured program that will help you develop properly. This is an immense act of your free will. Choose life. Choose to be all in. Choose to say yes to discipline, yes to guidelines, yes to instruction.

Your choice affects not only the quality of your own life but Cora's as well. It affects everyone who loves you. You do not have to live your life confused, angry, anxious, depressed, unable to maintain healthy relationships, unable to manage life, impulsive, always hustling. You can be strong, peaceful, wise, loving, disciplined, joyful, and prosperous, a great father and an extraordinary partner. You can make me so happy, too. I will be happy to see you happy. I will be heartbroken if you choose the way of your dad. You have the power to stop the generational curse with you. No more. You have the power to be clean, sober, faithful, and good. You have the capacity to create the best possible conditions for Cora to grow up. You have the power to choose well for Cora, so she will not have to endure the heartbreak that you and I have had to deal with. You can stop the suffering now. You can choose to do what you need to do so you can be in Cora's life. She needs you. You can choose so that Cora is only sad about not seeing you for a brief time in her life. Once you are healthy, restored, and able to function well, Cora can enjoy the security of her dad being there for her from age four, all the way through her school years, proms, holidays, ball games, her marriage, and her own children.

Your thoughts and your words are extremely powerful in directing the course of your life. I sent you a book by Joel Osteen, *I Declare: 31 Promises to speak over your life.*[21] Your words, especially those said aloud, are powerful. Say this out loud:

"I declare it is not too late to accomplish everything God has placed in my heart. I have not missed my window of opportunity. God has moments of favor in my future. He is preparing me right now because He is about to release a special grace to help me accomplish that dream. This is my time. This is my moment. I receive it today! This is my declaration. I declare that God has a great plan for my life. He is directing my steps. And even though I may not always understand how, I know my situation is not a surprise to God. He will work out every detail to my advantage. In His perfect timing, everything will turn out right. This is my declaration. I declare that God is bringing about new seasons of growth. I will not get stagnant and hold on to the old. I will be open to change, knowing God has something better in front of me. New doors of opportunity, new relationships, and new levels of favor are in my future. This is my declaration. I declare everything that doesn't line up with God's vision for my life is subject to change. Sickness, trouble, lack, and mediocrity are not permanent. They are only temporary. I will not be moved by what I see but by what I know. I am a victor and never a victim. I will become all God has created me to be. This is my declaration."

Daniel, when you go before the judge on March 29th, humble yourself. Say, "I was a fool. My thinking was all messed up. I am so sorry. I don't want to be a guy like that. I want to be a good man, a man of integrity. I want to be a good dad to my daughter. If you are willing to let me, I want to go to Adult/Teen Challenge for twelve months. I will commit to giving all that I have to the program to figure out how I ended up in this mess and to learn how to live my life well."

Know that you are deeply loved forever and always.

Mom

The Lord will work out his plans for my life—for your faithful love, O Lord, endures forever. (Psalm 138:8 NLT)

CHAPTER
5

EMOTIONS

Any person capable of angering you becomes your master.

~ Epictetus

My dear Daniel,

I heard a life-changing message this morning. It was about anger. Anger destroys the one who is angry and inflicts torment on those around him. To be free from anger—to be completely free from the destructive force of anger—you must talk. Tell the truth. Admit anger controls you. Find a trusted wiser mentor and be vulnerable. You will not die from vulnerability. You will be set free through vulnerability. A person can die from anger but not vulnerability. An angry person pushes people away. An angry person is lonely. My prayer for you is that all the hurt, all the anger, all the disappointment will be gone from your life and it will be replaced with peace, wisdom, patience, and true strength. Vulnerability is not weakness. It is an act of courage. A simple man hides behind anger and control. A wise man acknowledges his need for freedom from anger and control. He is willing to dig deep into the source of his anger. Then he is truly strong.

Anger is weakness. Anger causes one to lose jobs, relationships, and opportunities. Anger precedes evil, a will to harm another for wounding one's ego. We have a society that is addicted to anger and its more sinister cousin, contempt. Both of these emotions disregard the inherent worth of the other person. I grieve over the ridiculous television news talk shows whose participants scream over each other with ever-increasing levels of contempt. It accomplishes nothing of value. In fact, it opens the door to violence. Verbal violence nearly always precedes physical violence.

Self-control is power. Trying to control others is cruel. Compassion is strength. Forgiveness sets you free. Remember that people who have hurt you were hurt themselves. They too were lost, confused, scrambling to try to live but were unable to because of their own pain. Behavior flows automatically from our belief system. If a person is angry and violent, his behavior stems from the belief that others are out to get him. It is a fear-based existence. When you learn to believe what is true, accurate, and virtuous, then your behavior shows it.

There is a very helpful word to learn: *dikaiosune* (pronounced dik-ah-yos-oo'-nay). It is, in a broad sense, the state of a person who is as he or she ought to be. This person has integrity, virtue, purity of life, and correctness of thinking, feeling, and acting. To aspire to this requires a transformation of the heart. You may have heard it said, "Out of the abundance of the heart, one speaks." If anger, contempt, and blame spew from someone's mouth, you can quickly discern the condition of his heart—or soul. If patience, compassion, or love flow from someone, you can quickly discern the condition of his heart, too. I've told you before that a bad tree cannot produce good fruit.

The fruit of the Spirit is love, joy, peace, patience, kindness and self-control. Ask God to soften your heart, take away the anger, and fill your heart with peace, understanding, and compassion. Humble yourself, be teachable, admit your neediness—God's strength is made perfect in our weakness—when we acknowledge that apart from Him, we can do nothing. The good news is God loves that prayer. God loves a contrite heart. God loves for us to be truthful, admit our power-lessness and ask Him to take control—to show you who you are—to reveal His love and power that will propel you to your God-given destiny—an abundant life of love, joy, peace, patience, kindness, and service which is true strength: a man's man.

Know that you are deeply loved. I am excited about your future. You will discover gifts and talents that you didn't even know you had. God will take you places you never dreamed. You are blessed, gifted, a masterpiece, one of a kind, beautiful, strong, peaceful, smart, and in a position to get on the right path that will lead you to greater love, greater peace, greater prosperity, greater honor, and greater service to others.

I have amazing news! I know that God is going before you to open the way. I called Adult/Teen Challenge and spoke with the admission coordinator. He is holding a bed for you! Normally, it takes an application process, an interview, and waiting for a decision on acceptance!

He is going to call your lawyer and send her a letter that you have been accepted. He knows the judges in Dallas County and he told me they know the great success

Adult/Teen Challenge has, so it is looking very hopeful that you will not have to go to state prison. We are praying for a merciful judge.

This next year can be the best year of your life. Finally, you will be gaining understanding and wisdom, and receiving practical teaching and mentoring on who you are, why you're here, and what you are supposed to do in your life.

I love you forever and always. Stay strong. Stay humble. Pray. Listen. Be peaceful. Trust that God is working all things out for your good. He will do immeasurably, above and beyond what we can ask or think.

Mom

STRUGGLING TO BELIEVE

Dear Mom,

I stared at this blank page for an hour before something worth writing on it came to mind. I am reading I Corinthians right now. In one place it says "Stop deceiving yourselves. If you think you are wise by this world's standards, you need to become a fool to be truly wise." (I Cor. 3:18 NLT)

I know that it's probably pretty ignorant for me to 'all of a sudden' become a believer, and only start to follow God when times get hard, or I make a mistake and need "Him" to bail me out…so I'm trying to just take it slow, reading the Bible, praying, and seeing which verses speak to me or relate to my life right now.

I can't lie to myself or God and act like I completely believe or know that I need to dedicate myself to it. I guess I was only pushing it away because it was being pushed onto me so much. But you're right, and you have been right the entire time, that He is present and always has been. I still don't know what to make of this, all these new feelings of me wanting to increase the depths of my faith, but I know that I need to.

I know it's the best option for me right now and that I can't do much without Him. I never understood why or how someone could put so much faith into something so questionable. (I hope I'm making sense.)

But now, I see that everything really does happen for a reason and that it's more than just being a good person to believe and actually put things into God's hands. God is everything. I can't do anything without Him. I can only get so far in life by myself.

I've been so judgmental towards religion. I guess it really took me realizing that I'll never reach my full potential without Him. I haven't been dealt the best hand in life when it comes to my own personal decisions, my dad's issues and the relationship I had with him growing up, or how I neglected to take care of my own family when I had the chance to. But I really do see now that all of that would have been a lot easier if I had God in mind during that time. I always thought that I could just do it on my own.

I am very thankful that you are present in my life, Mom. I couldn't do anything without you. You are the only person that I can confide in and have always been the one person that I could ever really trust. And now, in what I would easily consider to be the hardest time of my life, you are still here for me and guiding me to God. Thank you so much.

When Terry told me that you did not want to talk to me or have anything to do with this situation, I was legitimately heartbroken because I understood that I had broken your heart. I couldn't eat or sleep, and I was always sick the first five days I was here.

Thank you so much for staying in my corner. You and Cora are the two people I love most and could not live without. (and grandma and papa too).

In closing, thank you also for continuing to try to show me God. Now I see that you always know best. I love you and I am looking forward to the day that I can make you happy. Everything you say sticks, bounces around, and echoes in my head until I really get it. I'm thankful for that and for you.

Jail is not teaching me the lesson I needed to learn. I am completely against the system of incarceration and probation. What's teaching me the lesson that I was ignoring is you and God. Now, being locked in a box, away from family and friends, certainly is helping me to see another side of life that I know is not me or anything that I want any part in.

But I now understand what I could not see before I got in this mess. I know what I need to be doing at this point in my life and to make better decisions. I want so badly to take back this mistake and do better as soon as I have that opportunity. I will make you proud of me and I will take care of my family. I love you so much. Everything is going to be all right.

Daniel

DOES THE BIBLE REALLY HAVE WISDOM FOR CREATING A LIFE OF JOY AND EXCELLENCE?

Mom,

You came and saw me today and gave me so much hope for the future. I know I probably seemed a bit detached from the world, for that I am sorry. These walls are starting to get to me but when you come see me, you seem to clear all of that away. You are completely right, everything is going to be better than ever when this is behind me. I love you and I am so thankful for you. I am so happy to be your son and I can't wait to make you happy and proud. I know this has to be as stressful, or more so, for you as it is for me. That's another reason that I'm so thankful that I still have you in my corner. I love you. Please give papa and grandma a hug and tell them I love them. The Bible is beginning to come alive to me. Here is what I read today:

Ephesians 3:17-19 (TLB): "And I pray that Christ will be more and more at home in your hearts as you trust in Him. May your roots go down deep into the soil of God's marvelous love. And may you have the power to understand, as all God's people should, how wide, how long, how high, and how deep His love really is. May you experience the love of Christ, though it is so great you will never fully understand it. Then you will be filled with the fullness of life and power that comes from God."

Isaiah 38:17 (TLB): "Yes, it was good for me to suffer this anguish, for You have rescued me from death and have forgiven all my sins."

Psalms 13 (TLB): "O Lord, how long will You forget me? Forever? How long will You look the other way? How long must I struggle with anguish in my soul, with sorrow in my heart every day? How long will my enemy have the upper hand? Turn and answer me, O Lord my God! Restore the sparkle to my eyes, or I will die. Don't let my enemies gloat, saying, 'We have defeated him!' Don't let them rejoice at my downfall. But I trust in Your unfailing love. I will rejoice because You have rescued me. I will sing to the Lord because He is good to me."

Daniel

Don't Put It Off

2 Peter 1:3-4 tells us that "everything that goes into a life of pleasing God has been miraculously given to us by getting to know, personally and intimately, the One who invited us to God. The best invitation we ever received! We were also given absolutely terrific promises to pass on to you—your tickets to participation in the life of God after you turned your back on a world corrupted by lust." (2 Peter 1:3-4 MSG)

Peter continues in verses 5-9: "So don't lose a minute in building on what you've been given, complementing your basic faith with good character, spiritual understanding, alert discipline, passionate patience, reverent wonder, warm friendliness, and generous love, each dimension fitting into and developing the others. With these qualities active and growing in your lives, no grass will grow under your feet, no day will pass without its reward as you mature in your experience of our Master Jesus. Without these qualities you can't see what's right before you, oblivious that your old sinful life has been wiped off the books." (2 Peter 1:5-9 MSG)

WRESTLING WITH DESPAIR

Mom,

Whenever I lay down to go to sleep, my mind starts to race. That's usually when I pull out this pen and paper. It's hard not to be anxious and scared for the outcome of this situation I've put myself in. I'm doing my best to pray and leave it in God's hands. When I lay down and my mind starts to race, it's not always about negative things. A lot of the things I think about (when I'm really trying to keep my mind blank so that I can sleep) are the main things that keep me going every day and keep me positive.

Your words of wisdom tend to be the majority of it. Speaking positivity into action every day, praying hard and keeping faith, that God will allow me to go to Adult/ Teen Challenge and make a better man of myself, and thinking very hard on the actions that put me here in the first place and how I can avoid them when I'm back home.

Not a single breath of yours, or a single word spoken or typed is going to waste. I think about every single bit of it, Mom. In a lot of ways, I thank God for giving me this opportunity to "fix" my life. I obviously wish it wasn't under these exact bad circumstances, but I know that when I have the chance, I'm going to be the best man, father, son, and overall person that I can be. The person I am meant to become. I love you so much. I love Cora and my dad and grandma and Papa

Charlie, and Papa and Linda and Aunt Sue and my family so much and I never want to let you guys down again, ever.

I want so badly for this chance to do right. Deep in my heart, underneath all the stress and the worry, I really do know that God has my back, and I will get the chance to make my family and everyone around me proud.

I'm sweating and nervous only because I know that this really is a deep hole I dug for myself and it's make or break for the rest of my life. But, like I said, I know God has got me. And I'm so excited to make something great for myself, finally. You and your wise words get me through every single day and the nights that I can't sleep. I love you.

Daniel

Mom,

Please read chapter 18 in the book of Matthew. It's been on my mind a lot lately that Rocky and Terry, my old room-mates, are avoiding me, and I really don't understand why, or what I did to deserve it. It really does break my heart that I don't have anything left at all. No clothes. No sentimentalism, nothing I've tried so hard to keep is left. It's all gone. I was always a loyal friend to them. God has been putting it on my heart to forgive them and to forget about all that stuff and move forward without it, but I'm finding that is harder than it seems. The day that I'm released from here, I would like to go there with you by my side, one single last time, just to ask why and to see if they still have any of my things. If they don't answer or if they shut the door in my face, I'll move on without a second thought, but I really feel it's worth one last effort.

On another note, I am finding that I cannot do time very well. I don't belong in jail and I feel extremely out of place here. I am very sad every night that I have to sleep here and when I wake up, it's even more of a mood killer to see the same sights, to wake up and herd like cattle to a line for a tray of food I would never even think of eating if I saw it out there in "the world."

It gradually gets harder and harder to keep my patience, to continue to remind myself that it's only temporary and to stay peaceful in a place that is the total and utter opposite of what I want to be. The simple things that keep me going are talking to you on the phone, looking through my pictures of family, and eating my fill in sweets that I know are defeating the purpose of me even working out, and still I find it hard. Still, I always go back to my bunk and want to cry or to punch a wall for no good reason. I hate this place. I never want to come back to jail. It's more than "learning my lesson." It's more that I don't have the faith right now or the strength to power through this every day. I know in my heart that I couldn't do a long stint of time. I am not made for this stuff. I guess it's God telling me that I need to keep on a straight path and do right, or this is what I'll be looking at.

I know this letter is very negative and I'm sorry for that. That wasn't my intention when I sat down to write it. I just have so much I want to say and to get off my chest, and I'm very stressed out, so the negative tends to come first.

I love you, Mom. I miss my life. I miss having Cora every other weekend. I can't wait to hold my daughter again. When I heard her voice, even though only for a split second, I teared up and got sucked deep into my feelings. This place teaches you to hide your feelings, to put a wall up.

I can't wait to hug you. I just want to be a decent father to Cora and a good son to you. I hope and pray every day that I can go home soon and get this show on the road. I'm more than ready. Please send me pictures of Cora in a letter (It has to be a letter, not by themselves or they will send them back. I don't know why.)

I love you, mom.

Daniel

PS Mom, please read this story about forgiveness

A STORY ABOUT FORGIVENESS

Matthew 18:21-35: At that point Peter got up the nerve to ask, "Master, how many times do I forgive a brother or sister who hurts me? Seven?" Jesus replied, "Seven! Hardly. Try seventy times seven. The kingdom of God is like a king who decided to square accounts with his servants. As he got under way, one servant was brought before him who had run up a debt of a hundred thousand dollars. He couldn't pay up, so the king ordered the man, along with his wife, children, and goods, to be auctioned off at the slave market. The poor wretch threw himself at the king's feet and begged, 'Give me a chance and I'll pay it all back.' Touched by his plea, the king let him off, erasing the debt. "The servant was no sooner out of the room when he came upon one of his fellow servants who owed him ten dollars. He seized him by the throat and demanded, 'Pay up. Now!' The poor wretch threw himself down and begged, 'Give me a chance and I'll pay it all back.' But he wouldn't do it. He had him arrested and put in jail until the debt was paid. When the other servants saw this going on, they were outraged and brought a detailed report to the king. The king summoned the man and said, 'You evil servant! I forgave your entire debt when you begged me for mercy. Shouldn't you be compelled to be merciful to your fellow servant who asked for mercy?' The king was furious and put the screws to the man until he paid back his entire debt. And that's exactly what my Father in heaven is going to do to each one of you who doesn't forgive unconditionally anyone who asks for mercy."

I love you, Mom. I miss you. I am so thankful for you and everything you do for me. I don't know what I would do without you. I can't wait to make you proud for a change.

I miss you very much, and I love you even more.

Daniel

Dear Daniel,

I received this message today from a dear friend in Washington. She, along with many others, is continually praying for you, Daniel.

"Good morning Deb,

I am sitting still and prayerfully listening for Jesus' words that are the ones that are worth waiting for. I know He is with you and the Holy Spirit is lovingly hovering over Daniel (as well as in him) to fan the flame of love in him. I keep having the thought that Daniel's discouragement is a place that God wants to "re-interpret" for him. Shame always wants to shout the last word with the aim of enslaving us and making us afraid and withdrawn among other things, and it is hard to hear Jesus' words: "Just come to Me with the weight of all your burdens. . . just as you are. I have words that will make a difference. Let Me have the last word!" Perhaps Daniel will discover and experience the God-given gift of genuine contrition that makes the way for a truly life-giving and freeing gratitude and humility even while he is in jail. I am praying that in this very place (emotionally, mentally, and spiritually, as well as the physical place he is in), he will experience the love of God and the disarming of the power of fear over his life. Maybe this is part of God's rescue. I am also praying for you, dear Momma. May God strengthen your heart to stand with your son in this painful place and to trust God that his suffering will be redemptive!

Lovingly, *Another Momma*"

And another note, this one from Brenda:

"Deb,

We stand steadfast in faith asking God to 'Do it again'! We cry out for Mercy over Justice! Father God, we lean not to our own understanding but in all our ways and thoughts we acknowledge YOU as Daniel's deliverer, redeemer, and savior. We cry with a loud united voice—Holy is the Lord God almighty! Mighty to save, deliver, and heal. Strength and honor belong to our God!

Father, we ask for You to speak to the attorneys and Judge what is YOUR perfect will for Daniel. We bind the Spirit of Confusion and Strife. We bind Legalism. We loose the Spirit of Life and Liberty over the proceedings and outcome. We ask for an Open Heaven over Daniel. For him to be steadfast, peaceful and humble in Your sight. Draw Daniel's heart close to You. We ask for divine favor and protection over Daniel. Thank You for never leaving us or forsaking us! We surrender Daniel to You once again to have Your will in his life. Thank You that nothing can stop the thought and plans You have for Daniel. We give You praise and adoration in all things.

In Jesus' Name, Amen
Brenda"

Greetings, Dear Friends,

I received a letter today from Daniel. It starts, "Mom, last night I had a dream about a church and a lot of people in a circle, and that's all that I remember from it, but I think it was me at Teen Challenge. I know it sounds cheesy, but I woke up excited that it might have been a sign that I'll be going there soon."

On a phone call with Daniel this morning, he said he has another court date on April 20th. I don't have any more details yet. I woke up with dark thoughts this morning but refused to let them take root. In hindsight, I wish I had had more poise and eloquence, but the truth is, mixed with raw emotion, muddled thoughts, fiery darts, sweat and tears, sometimes my faith walk is really messy.

Wholeheartedly grateful to all of you,
Deb

ANGER TOWARD WEAK MEN

Dear Daniel,

We are praying for mercy so that you can get to Teen Challenge right away. That is where you will learn who you are, come to know the voice of the Holy Spirit, and become all that God has created you to be. But even now, behind bars, you can still surrender your will to the One who knows you perfectly, loves you unconditionally, speaks to you in your inner man with holy whispers, and who alone can get you to where you need to be spiritually, physically, mentally, financially, and emotionally. It is the Holy Spirit alone who imparts truth, wisdom, counsel, comfort, and power. It is absolutely amazing to me that He gives us peace even in the midst of a storm. Trust Him in all things. He is God. He is spirit. He is a person. Who can understand such things apart from the Holy Spirit revealing this through scripture and actual experience? It is written that those who do not have the Spirit see such things as foolishness. I know I did before surrendering my life to Jesus. Then, it is as if my eyes were opened. My desires changed, my hope and joy became very real motivators, and a peace that came from finally understanding that I didn't have to figure life out on my own came so sweetly and surely. This is not a religious experience. I hate religion—a man-made structure of rules. I love the reality of a personal relationship with the spirit of life in Christ Jesus.

I must admit I am a bit angry today. Even so, my hope is in the goodness of God. He understands grief and loves me none the less despite my weakness. Oh, that we all might know and experience this love that surpasses understanding!

The anger I feel today is probably from fatigue, from wishing your dad was stronger, healthier, more faithful, to do the things that a father should do. He needs to visit you, put money on your account, encourage you, speak to the lawyers, etc. When men fail to step up to their God given responsibilities, it falls on women to do it all. Women are made to nurture; men are to provide, protect, and contend for their families. I encourage you to extend grace to Morgen. Nobody is perfect, but you must give her appreciation for providing for Cora alone. When we women have to do both roles, it can make us tough, overly protective, and sometimes angry. It is very hard when the man fails to do his part and it falls on us to do our best to do it all. Your anger at Morgen is displaced. Look at it from her perspective. Watch your words carefully. Speak well of her. Your words are creative. Do you want Cora to have a blessed mom or a cursed mom? Bless her. Appreciate her. Thank her. Honor her. Ask her forgiveness. Promise to do better. You can love her into being the woman God created her to be. Keep the door open for God to restore your family. God can do amazing things in transforming willing people into incredible testimonies of his grace. It is not too late for you to have an intact family. What a blessing if Cora could be raised by both her mom and dad! This can only be accomplished by the power of Christ. He can make all things new. He is the one that heals, restores, corrects our thinking, and reveals our arrogance-blame-anger cycle that keeps us stuck. It is Christ in you who will enable you to forgive, to accept responsibility for your part, and to love, protect, and provide.

Part of my grief is missing Cora. This is supposed to be the best part of my life, when I can be a grandma. Ask God to restore your family. Anything is possible with God. If He does it, it will be the most beautiful, blessed, loving relationship ever!

Psalm 27:11-14 pleads "Teach me how to live, O Lord. Lead me along the path of honesty, for my enemies are waiting for me to fall. Do not let me fall into their hands. Yet I am confident that I will see the Lord's goodness while I am here in the land of the living. Wait patiently for the Lord. Be brave and courageous. Yes, wait patiently for the Lord."

In Psalm 32:8, God promises to steer us: "I will guide you along the best pathway for your life. I will advise you and watch over you."

Psalm 33:18-22 speaks of His protection: "But the Lord watches over those who fear Him, those who rely on His unfailing love. He rescues them from death and keeps them alive in times of famine. We depend on the Lord alone to save us. Only He can help us, protecting us like a shield. In Him our hearts rejoice, for we are trusting in His holy name. Let your unfailing love surround us, Lord, for our hope is in You alone."

He also promises to always hear us in Psalm 34:4-10: "I prayed to the Lord, and He answered me, freeing me from all my fears. Those who look to Him for help will be radiant with joy; no shadow of shame will darken their faces. I cried out to the Lord in my suffering, and He heard me. He set me free from all my fears. For the angel of the Lord guards all who fear Him, and He rescues them. Taste and see that the Lord is good. Oh, the joys of those who trust in Him! Let the Lord's people show Him reverence, for those who honor Him will have all they need. Even strong young lions sometimes go hungry, but those who trust in the Lord will never lack any good thing."

The psalmist gives us his wisdom in verses 11-15: "Come, my children, and listen to me, and I will teach you to fear the Lord. Do any of you want to live a life that is long and good? Then watch your tongue! Keep your lips from telling lies! Turn away from evil and do good. Work hard at living in peace with others. The eyes of the Lord watch over those who do right; His ears are open to their cries for help."

The psalmist knows well how God rescues us and testifies to that in verses 17-18: "The Lord Hears His people when they call to Him for help. He rescues them from all their troubles. The Lord is close to the brokenhearted; He rescues those who are crushed in spirit."

Psalm 37:3-5 tells us of His promises: "Trust in the Lord and do good. Then you will live safely in the land and prosper. Take delight in the Lord, and He will give you your heart's desires. Commit everything you do to the Lord. Trust Him, and He will help you."

March 29th is the court date when Daniel will be sentenced for the aggravated robbery charge. I have to remind myself to breathe. The judge's decision is enormous for Daniel's future. I wrote this letter to the judge on the day before his court date:

Honorable Judge Holmes,

I am writing to you regarding my only son, Daniel James Peters III, who will appear before you tomorrow, March 29th at 9:00AM. I know the charge he faces is serious. I am heartbroken by his actions but extremely hopeful because of his brokenness, remorse, and sincere desire to learn what drove him to act out in a way that is totally contrary to who he is.

Daniel has struggled with his identity for some time. Although he is kind, compassionate, very smart, and loving, at times his anxiety and depression led him to self-medicate with marijuana, Xanax, and alcohol.

Daniel comes from a family of teachers, ministers, counselors, and small business owners—all of whom who see their work as sacred service to others. We love Daniel because we know who he really is and have had unwavering belief that he, too, will come to understand his true identity. We are people of faith who believe Daniel has a God-given destiny. Grandparents, cousins, mom, a former employer will all be in court tomorrow to support Daniel and to pray for mercy.

I believe Daniel's struggles stem from feelings of abandonment and shame because of his abusive, drug-addicted father, a successful businessman who got lost in his own dysfunction and lost everything. As so many young men do, Daniel desperately sought his dad's approval. Daniel is twenty-one now and has realized that his need for love and belonging cannot be met by his biological father, but it can be met by seeking God as Father. It can be met by the staff at Adult/Teen Challenge who stand ready to receive him, love him, teach him, and father him.

Adult/Teen Challenge of Texas is a twelve-month residential program that takes young men from hopelessness to purposefulness, addiction to freedom, brokenness to reconciliation. The resulting radical transformation leads many to pursue careers in ministry and in other helping professions after graduation.

Rehabilitation and redemption at Adult/Teen Challenge is far superior to punishment in prison. The sooner he gets to Teen Challenge the better. The staff of counselors is highly skilled and experienced in the areas of expertise Daniel needs. They have knowledge and experience in teaching life skills, managing probation requirements, and establishing young men on a solid foundation from which they can lead successful, meaningful lives of service. The success rate of the men's program at Teen Challenge is far superior to other programs, certainly far superior to Cenicor, The Substance Abuse Felony Punishment Facility (SAFPF), or prison.

I ask you, Judge Holmes, to see Daniel's brokenness and to see what Daniel will become, not only what he has done.

I have been a psychology professor and counselor for thirty-five years. I assure you if I believed Daniel was a danger to anyone I would not make this request. He is genuinely broken and eager to submit himself to mentoring by the men at Adult/Teen Challenge and to learn all he can about who he is, what he loves, what his

gift is, and how to live. Respectfully, I hope in this case mercy will triumph over judgment.
Wholeheartedly,
Debra Yoder, Ed.D. LPC-S, CDWF
Daniel's mom

Dear Deb,
It is scary to be in a trial with so much at stake. You are a wise momma who is standing by your troubled son as well as helping him to get to a place where rehabilitation is likely. How can that not be recognized as a good option to the judge when prison usually doesn't "teach" much that is good? We are praying, dear sister.
Jenny

Debby,
We are praying for you right now. We know court is about to start. We asked that God would be with you, that you would lean on him, for the judge to have a kind and open heart, for the Teen Challenge guy to speak clearly, and for the prosecutor to have an open heart or else have garbled words. Keep us in the moment. Let us know what is happening.
Jane

The morning of the trial was so tense. I was in a daze driving to the courthouse. Seeing all of Daniel's cousins, his grandparents, Morgen's dad, my best friend and her husband broke down whatever emotional steel I had mustered. We filled one side of the court room. An inmate was brought in from a side door dressed in orange prison clothes with chains on his wrists and ankles. There was nobody there in the gallery for him. He was totally alone. The prosecutor and defense attorney spoke to the judge about the man as if he was not even there. They determined his sentence without a word from him. His eyes were lifeless, as if he had been under someone else's control for much of his life. "Six years!" Slam of the gavel. He shuffled out the side door shadowed by two armed officers. Two more inmates went through very much the same experience. No family. No friends. All alone. One was like the first, defeated and lifeless. The third was cocky and arrogant and had to be restrained by the officers. My heart broke for all of them. What had gone so wrong in their lives that they ended up here alone and without hope?

Daniel entered the courtroom as the three before him had, orange garb, chains on his wrists and ankles. My heart sank. How did we get here? What went so wrong? Oh God, have mercy on Daniel. Rescue him from the fate of the men before him.

Daniel's lawyer questioned Daniel, Morgen's dad, and the advocate for Adult/Teen Challenge. Then the prosecutor stood. We were told she was hard and would not agree to a lesser sentence than five years in state prison. I could not breathe.

Then she spoke. "Daniel, are all these people here to support you?"

"Yes, ma'am."

The energy in the room shifted immediately. She began to scold him like a mother and insisted that if he had the chance to go to a program like Adult/Teen Challenge rather than prison, he sure better get his act together and stop acting like a fool. It sounded as if she was arguing FOR him. Within minutes, the judge agreed to twelve months at Adult/Teen Challenge and five years' probation. I think I was down the hall and out of the courthouse before realizing what had just happened. Oh my! Daniel is going to be all right! I sent a text to the friends standing with us across the country:

Dear friends,

Wow! The angel was the prosecutor! She sounded like an advocate, a mother, a defender! Adult/Teen Challenge is approved! Five years of probation. No jail time! He could have been sentenced to five to ninety-nine years! I think the prosecutor was touched by the overwhelming presence of all of us there to support Daniel. Grandma, papa, most of his cousins, Anna, Jessica, Daven, Chris, Greg, and more. We filled one side of the court room! Daniel was certainly touched when he walked in the courtroom in chains and glanced at his whole extended family there, praying and loving him. I am sure he felt a mix of shame and gratitude. Daniel will be transferred to the Tarrant County Jail to face the charges there. Oh, for more mercy that they too will agree to Adult/Teen Challenge and probation!

Gratefully, *Deb*

Deb, an angel impersonating the prosecutor! The lengths God goes to reach over the edge for lost lambs!!!!

Hallelujah!!!! *Jenny*

It would be weeks before Daniel would be transferred to the Tarrant County Jail. His next letters after the verdict were a bit more encouraging.

Mom,

I just finished eating a tray with a taco, some beans, rice, and two cookies on it. They call it "Taco Bell" here. I can't wait to actually eat something from Taco Bell. I'll never eat another ramen noodle soup again.

I think everybody has a limit to how long they can put up with this place, some a lot more than others. I think I've hit my limit. All I can think about is going home. I just want so badly to relax at your house with Cora for a day or two before I have to go to Adult/Teen Challenge, to eat breakfast, watch television, and sit on your patio. I just want to play with Cora on your living room floor one more time before I'll only be able to see her at a visitation for the next year. I miss her so much and that's all I think about that makes me happy in here . . .thinking about hugging you and holding Cora and being "free" again. I really hope Teen Challenge gives me the opportunity to see Cora and you as often as possible, and I really hope it's actually as livable as it seems. I just want to be out there in the sunlight so badly. I miss you so much. I love you so much.

Daniel

Mom,

Last night I had a dream about a church and a lot of people in a circle, and that's all that I remember from it. But I think it was me at Teen Challenge. I know it sounds cheesy, but I woke up excited that it might have been a sign that I'll be going there soon. I sure am sick of being here.It makes a huge difference when I am exercising, when I have some stuff in my bag to eat, and when I have a good book to read. You make all that possible. Thank you so much! I love you.

I've written three or four letters to Chris, Morgen's dad, but I can't find it in myself to send them out. They're very personal and when I read them back after writing them, I always end up throwing them away. I really just want to apologize and thank him. It's a lot for him to still be here for me when his daughter doesn't even want to. It breaks my heart that I can't talk to Cora and tell her I love her every night. I hope that changes soon. I hope Morgen lets down this wall that I've forced her to put up. I miss her and Cora.

I'm so thankful to be your son, Mom. You really are the best person in the world. Whenever I'm in a bad mood or I get in my feeling, especially in here, it doesn't take anything but hearing your voice to put me in a better mood and to make me re-think where I stand and that it could be worse, always. I also want you to know that you are the only one who answers the phone every single time that I call, and that makes a huge thing when I really got to thinking about it. Because it has always been that way. You have always had my back, and I can't say that about anyone else, anyone. I really look up to you more than anyone.

I can't wait to get out of here and make you proud. I think about it every single day. I miss you so much. I just want to hug you and I really want to spend time with you and Cora

together when I get out of here and before I go to Teen Challenge. I have five days and I want to spend three of them with Cora and you. I hope that it is very soon, very, very soon.
Daniel
PS I'm okay so don't worry too hard.

ENCOURAGEMENT FROM AUNT SUE

Deb,

What sweetness of God for Daniel to have that dream. We are warring with you for it to come to pass! God's mercies are new every morning -GREAT is His faithfulness. It is a huge battle for our thoughts not to be overcome with shame and failure. Thank God it is not about our ability but our yielding to let God be glorified through our weakness.

Psalm 51:17 says "The sacrifices of God are a broken spirit; A broken and a contrite heart, O God, You will not despise." Psalms 34:18 assures us that "The LORD is near to the brokenhearted and saves those who are crushed in spirit."

Weakness is uncomfortable, but we are all weak and in need of Jesus. I'm so proud of you and the truth is you are a fabulous teacher, mom, sister, friend, daughter, follower of Jesus as with us all with weakness. Don't let the devil magnify the pain – there is so much good! My motto this year is "good not perfect." Everyone has pain and failure. We need Jesus, and heaven is our real home. Let's all picture Daniel in a circle of Christians thriving at Teen Challenge.

I love you.
Sue

LEARNING TO APPRECIATE RATHER THAN COMPLAIN

Mom,

I've learned a lot in my stay here. Mostly, what I should have appreciated and what I did to end up here in the first place. Also, I learned the hundreds of different ways to cook ramen noodle soups and that I never want to eat another one again – gross! I've been thinking about what meal I'm going to want to eat the first day that I'm home. It's a tie between Griff's greasy burgers or steak. I really don't mind as long as it's REAL meat.

I've also learned while being here that I'm a lot more patient than a lot of people. I've seen people get into it over things that I've been putting up with since my first day here without complaining. I've seen guys my age practically go crazy because their mom or dad didn't come bail them out right away. I'm still not comfortable here nor do I ever want to get too comfy here, but it's nice to see that I'm doing better than most. I've also gained quite a bit of weight despite eating gross food. I feel good and healthy. I miss you every day. I miss Cora and papa and grandma and everyone. I'm looking forward to spending a couple days with you and Cora. I don't think it would have been healthy for me to go straight to Adult/Teen Challenge after spending this much time in jail. I need a break, a day or two just to hold Cora and eat good meals with you. Maybe we could go see a movie together.

I hope I will be on my way home on Thursday, but if not, I hope to be released soon. I'm hoping for the best but expecting the worst. I've been praying hard for mercy from the judges and probation department. I believe I will be home very soon, whether it be in three days or Thursday, which is probably the day you are reading this letter, or in a couple more weeks.

Everything will be all right. I truly believe that. I'm so thankful for you, Mom. I love you.

Daniel

ANOTHER VERDICT

Greetings, Friends,

Daniel's lawyer just called me. The prosecutor has offered the minimum of six months in state jail (for the Tarrant County probation violation charges). I asked her if she can argue for time served and the case be done. That would be best. Her response was a bit confusing in that it depends on whether the original probation sentence has expired or not. We want Daniel to get to Adult/Teen Challenge as soon as possible. I don't know what is best or what the legal restraints may be. Legalese has me a bit confused. The thought of him going to state prison is frightening. My hope is that his lawyer will do her best work ever, and somehow get him to Adult/Teen Challenge without delay. She will meet with Daniel and present the offer. She then meets with the prosecutor this Thursday, April 20th, to work out the best deal.

I know that God is good. He knows the best course and loves Daniel even more than we do. Your counsel on how I should pray is welcomed. Your prayer for Daniel is amazing. What God did for Daniel on the Dallas case was miraculous. He can do it again. Daniel's letters and phone calls continue to be encouraging. I believe his repentance is real and his desire for God is genuine.

I was encouraged yesterday when I received a text from Morgen asking how she might visit Daniel. They will be co-parenting Cora, so it is good that she is willing to build an amicable relationship. Thank you for caring, for reading my sometimes-desperate emails, and for praying.

Love you, *Deb*

CHAPTER
6

FAITH

Faith is to believe what you do not see;
the reward of this faith is to see what you believe.
~ Saint Augustine

Dear Daniel,

I continue to wait with hope for the day you will be released. I am anxious for you to be in a place where you can sit under sound teaching and be surrounded by people who love you and are solely dedicated to helping you learn who you are, discover your gifts, and most importantly teach you to hear God for yourself.

I imagine it is difficult to hold on to your dignity in jail where love is not the motivation, but punishment is. Don't allow your current circumstances to define you. Your identity is in Christ. That means you are of immense value. The plans He has for you are for a beautiful future.

For years, I knew about God but did not know Him as personal friend. Unfortunately, I had not seen much difference in people who called themselves Christians and the rest of us. I have since learned that too few people go beyond a superficial glance toward heaven. There is a vast difference between simply saying a prayer to receive forgiveness and becoming a disciple. Too many churches make converts but not disciples. It is tragic that most converts never experience real transformation, so they fail to gain the understanding, power, and insight to live their lives with clear purpose, true identity, and wisdom.

When we humble ourselves, put our trust in the unseen God, and ask the Holy Spirit to open our eyes and our hearts, an extravagant exchange takes place. The things that used to dominate our thinking begin to shift. Anger, frustration, demanding our own way, paranoid thinking, criticism and judgment of others, and the pursuit of self (usually in destructive ways) all lead to a pitiful, earthbound life. Our minds are darkened, carnal, and void of self-control. We are unable to receive love or give love from a pure heart. Since we think it is all about us, we cannot have genuine connection with others. We often mistreat others out of our own pain.

We are wired for love and belonging. We are made for connection. Selfishness blocks that possibility. Thinking too highly of oneself or thinking too lowly of oneself blocks that possibility.

It is by faith that we obtain these exceedingly great and precious promises. By faith, we say, "Lord, fill me with your Spirit; enlighten the eyes of my understanding, that I may have strength and wisdom to live my life well. Show me how to have genuine love connections with others."

It is by faith that we believe that we are completely forgiven when we ask for forgiveness. My favorite scripture is Romans 8:1-2: "There is no condemnation for those who are in Christ.

He has made us free from the law of sin and death and has translated us into a new life." By faith, we now have the right to ask for wisdom.

The extravagant exchange is motivated purely by love. Most people don't know what real love is. They think it is a feeling. Well, feelings come and go. I Corinthians 13 is the love chapter. It says love is patient and kind. Love is not jealous or boastful or proud or rude. Love does not demand its own way. Love is not irritable, and it keeps no record of when it has been wronged. It is never glad about injustice but rejoices whenever the truth wins out. Love never gives up, never loses faith, is always hopeful, and endures through every circumstance.

The Holy Spirit is at work in you helping you to love this way. Wherever it says love, replace it with your name and ask God to make this real in your life.

"Daniel is patient and kind. Daniel is not jealous or boastful or proud or rude. Daniel does not demand his own way. Daniel is not irritable, and he keeps no record of when he has been wronged. Daniel is never glad about injustice but rejoices whenever truth wins out. Daniel never gives up, never loses faith, is always hopeful, and endures through every circumstance."

Someone told me years ago about replacing the word "love" with your name in these verses. It is helpful. But more enlightening is to realize that it is our faith in the love of God to change us. So, if Father God is love, "Father God is patient and kind. Father God is not jealous or boastful or proud or rude. Father God does not demand His own way. Father God is not irritable, and He keeps no record of when He has been wronged. Father God is never glad about injustice but rejoices whenever truth wins out. Father God never gives up, never loses faith, is always hopeful, and endures through every circumstance."

Like Paul teaches in Romans 7: "15I don't really understand myself, for I want to do what is right, but I don't do it. Instead, I do what I hate . . . 24Oh, what a miserable person I am! Who will free me from this life that is dominated by sin and death? 25Thank God! He will!"

No amount of striving to be good or to do good will ultimately succeed. It is Christ in us who transforms us from selfish beings to loving beings. So, it seems to me that all we are required to do is believe: "Lord, I trust You to work love into my very being. I trust You, Holy Spirit, to manifest the fruit of Your spirit in my life. I can't do it on my own. Thank You that You will! I will do my part to seek You, talk to You, and read Your word and trust You to enable me to do what it says."

So, what does this mean in practical application? Consider your thoughts, words, and actions toward Morgen. Love will win. Love will result in the best possible outcome. Strife, blame, criticism, judgment, or bullying will never get the result you want. Persistent kindness, understanding, love, and patience will result in peace. To access and to manifest the spirit of God in you, choose to be mindful of His presence. A powerful prayer is, "Holy Spirit, help me. Enable me. Live through me. Love through me. I die to self, and the life I now live is Christ in me."

Daniel, the opportunity you have now to go to Adult/Teen Challenge is a wonderful gift. I wish I had learned the things you are going to learn there when I was your age. It would have saved a bunch of heartache. You are only twenty-one. It's a perfect time to turn things around.

There are countless stories of lives transformed from hopelessness to hope, from addiction to freedom, from violence to peace, and from depression to joy. Believe that it is possible to learn practical life skills and wisdom for living. Many have shown that it is indeed possible—even against seemingly insurmountable odds. There are extraordinary stories all around us. The first step is to believe it is possible. Hope has a way of opening the door through which the universe gladly pours provision for astonishing transformation. It opens the way where there seemed to be no way.

I love you Daniel! Forever and always! *Mom*

THE DIFFICULT DRIVE TO ADULT/TEEN CHALLENGE

Daniel was released from the Tarrant County jail in early July. He was able to come home for a week before turning himself in to Adult/Teen Challenge in Azle, Texas. I was no longer afraid of him, but I was still afraid for him. His old roommates lived within walking distance of my house. I begged him not to go over there. He did anyway. I don't know what happened there, but he came home with a trash bag full of some of his belongings. He was quiet that week. No angry outburst, no familiar profanity, just quiet and sad. His eyes were distant and confused. Cora stayed with us the last couple of days, and I was so pleased to see his gentleness with her.

The morning I drove him to Adult/Teen Challenge, I was on pins and needles. Would he go? The tension was palpable during the two-hour car ride. I had such hope that if I could just get him there and turn him over to these men who would teach him, he would be safe. I checked him in and could not hold back the tears. The relief, the grief, the gratitude for this place of refuge for him along with the fear that he would bolt, overcame any resolve I had to be peaceful and dignified. The men saw my pain and asked if we could pray. Holding hands in a circle right outside the entrance, they declared new beginnings for Daniel. I kept my eyes on Daniel. He was cold, hard, and angry like a bear caught in a trap. If he had spoken, I believe he would have sneered, "Okay, I will go through the motions of this stupid program because I have to, but they will never get to me."

I could barely see to drive down the two-lane country road back toward the interstate highway. Burning tears, moans of agony, of relief, of uncertainty scrambled my ability to think. I pulled over near a pasture and let grief have its way.

Arriving home, not really remembering how I got there, I fell across the bed and slept for several days straight. I had no idea the toll the many years of stress and struggle had taken on my mind and on my body.

NOW AT ADULT/TEEN CHALLENGE

Mom,

My first few days were okay. I think everything is going to be fine; in fact, I know it will be. I just want to thank you for this opportunity and everything that you do for me. I'm so incredibly thankful to have everything that I need while I'm here. It means a lot to me to know that I am loved so much by you.

I am looking forward to seeing you when I can have visits and I already miss you a ton. I miss Cora a ton, too. I am happy to tell you that I have not had a single bad experience or negative thought about the program, and I know I'm going to do just fine. The food is much better than jail and there is no shortage of it. They feed us just fine.

I wrote grandma a short letter and sent it with this one because I don't have her address, so please forward it. I love you and I miss you a ton. Everything is going to be all right.

Daniel

PS Send pictures of Cora and you and family. I forgot to bring any. Love you!

Mom,

I feel pretty good about the program. I'm not in love with the way they do things here, but it is definitely possible to put up with, and I do feel like I will learn some valuable key lessons I'll be able to apply to my life when I go home. It is hard not to think about what is going on at home, but I know I need to put those parts of my life on hold and focus on myself and my relationship with God.

I miss Cora a lot and I think that is the hardest part of being here. I miss you, too. I was told that we hold a church service every Thursday night at 7PM and that you could come and sit with me. If the drive isn't too hard and if you feel up to it, I would really enjoy it.

I'm going to take the hint I got from the ton of envelopes in my bag that you would like me to write you a lot, so I will. I love you, mom.

Daniel

PS Give papa a big hug for me please!

Dear Grandma,

I hope you are doing all right. I think about you every day and miss you. I love you. I am going to take this program one day at a time, and I am enjoying it so far. From my first couple of days, I think everything is going to be just fine! Thank you so much for the awesome Bible! I love that it is a parallel/amplified Bible, so I can understand it better. I love you and I am looking forward to coming home to visit for a few days in about six months and looking forward to completing the program in about a year. I know that I can do this. I love you so much. Miss you xoxo.

Daniel

PS I really enjoyed lunch with you and I'm happy I got to do that before I came here. Love you!

Hey, Grandma,

I hope everything is going okay at home. Everything is going okay here. I am comfortable and slowly but surely getting into the swing of things and the set schedule here. Today, I get to leave the campus with another guy and a pastor and go to a church or the pastor's house and help them with a small job. It takes most of the day and we get to eat out at a restaurant, so I'm looking forward to it. I miss you and love you. I will write you every time that I have something of substance to write about. Please give Papa Charlie a hug for me. Also, I enjoy when I am reading my Bible and I come across a verse that you have highlighted. It just makes it mean that much more. Thank you, again, for the Bible. I look forward to hearing from you.

Love,

Daniel

Mom,

I love you and I just want you to know that you are my guardian angel. I am enjoying this time I have to focus on myself and what I'm going to do differently when I come home. It's hard being away from home and being so out of control of everything. I hope everything is going well with your work and at home. I'm looking forward to seeing you and Cora at a visit soon.

Love you more than anything.

Daniel

Hey mom,

I love you and miss you. I hope everything is okay at home. I'm enjoying my time here and just taking it day by day. I was going to ask if you could send a lot of pictures of Cora, maybe some of Morgen, some of you and the rest of the family.

I also need a pair of tennis shoes and I was really hoping you wouldn't mind ordering my favorite pair and having them sent here, please? They are Nike Janowskis. I'll let you pick the color (anything but white). Thank you. They are just the most comfortable ever, and I figured since I'll have them for so long that would be all right. I love you. I hope everything is good at home and that Papa's flowers are doing good after all this rain today.

Write me back and please send a ton of pictures. I'll be able to call you in about a week.

I love you.

Daniel

Hey Mom,

I miss you and love you. I hope everything at home is going okay. I've been thinking a lot about my past and my youth because I realized I'm going to have to talk about some of it when I give my testimony. I realized I didn't forget a lot of things but just sort of blocked it out of my memory or tried not to think about some of it.

I was trying to think back in chronological order, starting at being born in Waco, living at that house with the two rooms upstairs, the two stairs going to the living room, the little play park thing in the backyard, and the weird driveway. I forgot what street it was on, so I guess that's the best way to describe it. Then my memory kind of jumps to living with you in Mission, Texas, then Austin, then to living in the house on Big Oaks with you. I remember going to see my dad on some weekends and going to live with him for a year or two, of course, but I was hoping you could maybe help me fill in some of the blanks. I want to know partly for my story and testimony I have to give and partly for my own understanding and to help me remember some things I may have left out or forgot.

I love you.

Daniel

PS I really enjoyed seeing you last week and wish I could have stayed longer and maybe talked about this when I was there with you. I hope to get a letter back from you soon. I'm looking forward to getting my shoes in the mail. Thank you so much. I love you.

REMEMBERING DANIEL'S PAST

Dear Daniel,

Thank you for your letters. I finally received the butterfly and wheat ones this week. Your artwork on the envelopes is absolutely beautiful. I am encouraged by your words of insight and the hope you have for your future. I don't have your password for your Instagram, so I couldn't print the pictures of Cora you requested. I'm looking forward to seeing you after phase one of the program. I am so grateful you are in a good place. I hope you are sincerely grateful always too because it could have been state jail time. When you change the way you look at a thing, the thing you're looking at changes. Be grateful. Be kind. Be patient. Be excellent. We can't change ourselves, but the Word of God and His love for us is always eager to make us more and more into who He created us to be. All we have to do is ask Him, relax, and believe He will.

This year you have the opportunity to develop patience, perseverance, tenacity, loyalty, faithfulness, kindness, compassion, and wisdom for life. Look for the good and you will always find it. Look for something to complain about and you will always find it. So, look for the good. Gratitude is the way of happiness. Complaining keeps you circling the same mountain of confusion, over and over.

My hope is that you will learn to love work, any kind of work. Do whatever you do with excellence and a good attitude. Promotion comes from having a good attitude regardless of the circumstance. Promotion comes from humility, working diligently, and having the courage to dig in and try new things. If you sweep the floor, do it better than everybody. If you are speaking, prepare well. If you are washing dishes, do it with excellence, leaving nothing undone. Look for ways to put a mark of excellence on it. Before I counsel a client, I say, "Holy Spirit, do what only You can do. Use me to help these people. In my own strength, I can do nothing significant. But You can through me. Let me hear Your voice before I speak so my words will be wise." Before I teach a class, I ask for His Anointing to magnify my effectiveness. It's amazing. Sometimes I leave a counseling session or a class and say to myself, "Wow! That was awesome! God, I love watching You work. What a privilege to be used by You."

When I try to make things happen on my own, it rarely turns out well. The Holy Spirit really does give us the power and the wisdom to make good decisions when we humble ourselves and ask Him. A beautiful life is the result of stringing together one right decision after another. I believe wholeheartedly that God has a specific plan for your life. He knows the place, time, people, career, timing, and skill set you will need. Ask Him to order your steps. Ask to be in

His perfect will. Through faith and patience, you will receive
the promise. You are already changing. Discipline never is
pleasant at the time, but it yields the peaceable fruit of righteousness. Relax and depend on God 100% to do the work in
you. He is the author and perfecter of your faith.

You asked about your life story. You remembered quite a
bit. You were born in Waco, planned for and wanted. I was so
very happy. You were dedicated to God in church there in
Waco when you were just a few weeks old. The pastor declared
over you, "Daniel is a man like Enoch who pleases God. Great
will be his peace." Your dad was happy about you too, but I
did not know at the time that he had a secret addiction to
cocaine. He was soon lost in that addiction and became
abusive and impossible to live with. He would say he would
change, even go the pastor, but he only got worse. He became
physically, emotionally, financially, and spiritually abusive. I
prayed for him to get help and change, but it became too
dangerous for me and for you.

There were horrendous episodes of his rage and craziness,
but you don't need to hear that and, frankly, I don't want to
relive it. Just know that Aunt Sue and Uncle Marty tried to
help him many times, often coming to rescue you and me in
the middle of the night from his terrorizing behavior. Finally
one night, the neighbors called the police and he was put in
jail. The next day, the church helped get you and me out into
a safe house. I believed marriage was a covenant not to be
broken, so I told God, "He will have to either kill me or divorce
me because I believe nobody is beyond redemption." In hindsight, I was quite foolish. I should have left the first time he hurt

me. Thankfully, God answered my prayer, and he divorced me. In my ignorance, God rescued me anyway.

We moved in with Brenda for five months, then Mom and Charlie for a few months until I could heal emotionally enough to function, get a job, and save enough money to get a place of our own. I rented a house and started back to work at Cedar Valley College at a job that I was way overqualified for. We had to eat, so I was grateful for any job. A year into that job, you were at your dad's for a weekend visit and his then-girlfriend called me, crying, saying, "Come and get Daniel. His dad just beat me up and I'm going to the police." I drove to Waco 100 miles an hour, picked you up, and vowed never to let you be exposed to that violence again, despite the court saying I had to allow you every-other-weekend visits with him.

I called a friend at South Texas College and asked for a job. He agreed, and I immediately moved you and me ten hours away to Mission, Texas. I loaded up a U-Haul, got our cocker spaniel Solomon, and we left without telling anyone. Your dad was dangerous, and I didn't want him to know where we were. You started pre-school and kindergarten in Mission. I was at work one day and you were at a Christian day care at the church we attended. The Hildalgo County sheriff came in my office, put handcuffs on me, and took me to jail. At that same moment, your dad was kidnapping you from the daycare. I was released within hours with no charges, and right away, I hired a lawyer to get you back. I was beside myself with fear. I feared for your safety. I knew he just wanted to hurt me. My dad and Aunt Sue would not allow me to go immediately to get you because they thought it was a trap. He kept you twelve days and called me and said, "Come and get Daniel. He misses you." I was so relieved that you were okay, and we went back to south Texas.

After two years there, we moved to Austin where I was accepted into a doctoral program. We were in Austin 2001-2003, when you were in first and second grade. Then we moved into an apartment in Dallas near grandma, and I went to work for Richland College. We moved to the house on Big Oaks in 2003. By the time you were ten in 2005, you were very difficult to handle. You had no respect for authority and had an explosive temper. The school called me almost daily. At home, you would go from being sweet into a rage instantly. I took you to doctors, counselors, pastors, and then finally to a Christian boarding school in San Marcos. You stayed one semester but had to leave because I could no longer afford it. I owed them over twenty thousand dollars.

When you were twelve, I could not handle you and reluctantly agreed for you to go live with your dad. By that time, he was remarried, and I hoped he had become more stable and civil. That didn't go as well as we hoped. You ended up in alternative school in Waco. Your dad took off to New Orleans and left you with his wife. I came and got you. We lived on Big Oaks and I continued to do the best I could with you. We had many happy days. You were baptized at church and went to youth activities occasionally. But there were also many days where you scared me with your rage. You were smoking marijuana and hanging around bad friends. You refused to do what I said. You quit swim team, baseball, soccer, and everything I had hoped would be good for you.

After you stole Linda's car, wrecked it, and spent time in juvenile detention, Uncle David agreed to have you come live with him in San Diego. I was hopeful and very relieved, because walking on egg shells around you was killing me. You were still very troubled while with David. He tried valiantly, even moving to an expensive neighborhood in San Diego, so you could go to the best school. You refused. You trashed his house, were utterly disrespectful to him, threatened to kill yourself, on and on. After a few months, David finally called me saying he couldn't do this anymore. It was killing him. I flew you back home. You dropped out of high school, continued smoking pot, and refused to take direction from me. I paid for you to finish high school online. It is kind of a blur after that. I think shortly after that, you moved in with Morgen.

I prayed over you constantly: "Daniel is a man like Enoch who pleases God. He is a man of peace." Through elementary school, I sang over you and with you every night, "There are angels round about our house. We know that they're here, can't see 'em with our eyes but we know that they're here. His banner over us is Jesus. His banner over us is love." Do you remember that?

Daniel, forgetting what lies behind, we press on to what lies ahead. All things become new. We all have sordid stories of a pitiful life lived prior to the transforming work of the Spirit. Doing life on our own without God is always unfulfilling, awful, arrogant, petty, and selfish. A bad tree cannot produce good fruit, hard as we try. We came from God, are sustained by God, and we will return to God. All that matters now is our life after we have received the Spirit of Life in Christ Jesus. This letter of your past is not meant to shame you or make you feel bad. We all have a story. We cannot change what we refuse to bring to the light. Now, the real story is being written. The letters from here on out from you and to you will tell of God's redeeming power. As your life in Christ grows stronger and stronger, it will tell an awesome, supernatural, amazing story. Your life will have an impact on others. It will give much needed hope to mothers and fathers praying for their sons and daughters. It will give hope to those still struggling with anger, addictions, and confusion. Oh, what a beautiful story it will be! It will still have struggles, but now with a skill set and practical wisdom for managing those struggles.

I don't know why you were troubled and angry. I did my best to find answers and help you. I could give you a psychological theory, such as abuse and abandonment by a father, an over-indulgent, over-protective, over-worked, tired, and depressed mother . . . but none of that explains it all. You were primarily raised by me, and you had it pretty good. But you did see your dad have uncontrolled anger, use drugs, and disrespect women, and you were subjected to his angry outbursts more often than he was instructive or nurturing to you.

Psychologically, I believe your dad suffers from narcissistic personality disorder. That is a mental disorder in which people have an inflated sense of their own importance, a deep need for admiration, and a lack of empathy for others. But behind this mask of ultra-confidence lies a fragile self-esteem that's vulnerable to the slightest criticism. Exacerbated by drugs, alcohol, and pornography, he has intermittent explosive disorder (IED) which involves repeated, sudden episodes of impulsive, aggressive, violent behavior or angry verbal outbursts in which he reacts grossly out of proportion to the situation. He goes into a rage at the slightest frustration. He started using drugs when he was quite young, and as is often the case, did not develop emotionally or socially beyond that age. A person's development stops when they alter their brain chemistry, especially by psychotropic drugs. But because he is smart and manipulative, he was able to hide it by his charm and intelligence for some time. However, drugs eventually took control. I am still saddened by the fact that if he had stopped drugs and submitted himself to discipleship that he could have realized his potential and had a happy life. Very sad.

Pride, shame, selfishness, and rejection of the Holy Spirit's correction to destructive thoughts, feelings, and behaviors is a very sad existence. Rebellion is like the sin of witchcraft and opens the door to demonic spirits to dominate a person's life. Rebellion against authority or social norms, thinking "the rules don't apply to me," is a dangerous path. Proverbs 17:13 NLT says, "If you repay evil for good, evil will never leave your house." Ephesians 6:4 NLT says, "Don't make your children angry by the way you treat them; rather, bring them up with the discipline and instruction approved by the Lord."

You were dedicated to God before birth and prayed over all your life. I believe we have an enemy that tried to take you out, but he was destined to fail. Although you have suffered much, now you have been saved. The process of sanctification has begun, and God will do immeasurably above and beyond what we could hope or ask in your life. It is all Him.

This morning I re-read the letters I wrote to you while you were in jail, along with a couple of letters I wrote to my friends who were faithfully praying for you throughout all this. I will send those to you. It may be helpful to you to read those in chronological order. I was amazed to see God's faithfulness day by day. At times, I wrote in desperation through tears. Other times my faith was strong. He indeed shows His strength in our weakness. Prayer is powerful—not always pretty and polished, but always powerful. Somehow, by the time our prayer reaches heaven, all God hears is "My child is in trouble." And He then moves heaven and earth to meet our need. Though our faltering words mix faith with doubt, hope with fear, and deep yearning with agony, all God hears is our heart crying, "Daddy, Abba, help me." The perfect father that He is moves mountains, crushes the opposition, and scoops us up to safety. Every time.

I can only imagine what was happening in the spirit during this time of travailing prayer for you. I believe there were dozens of warring angels descending from and ascending to heaven like bolts of lightning. I believe the Holy Spirit hovered over you, protecting you while you lay in your bunk in jail and easing your mind when fear, anger, and despondency crept in. I believe the accuser tried to make a case before God, and Jesus Himself interceded for you and claimed you as His own. I believe God Himself, said, "No, Satan. Daniel is my boy. He was dedicated to me from before he was born. He is a man like Enoch who pleases me. He is a man of peace. Get your hands off him!" I believe there were angels comforting me, strengthening me, and standing guard over me to prevent the accuser and faith-stealers from taking up residence in my thought life. I believe there was rejoicing in heaven when you received God's forgiveness and invited Jesus to take control of your life. I believe they threw a party in heaven, just as the father did when the prodigal son came home. The angels sang and danced, gave high fives, prepared a feast, and excitedly told the story of their victory.

I believe Satan and his defeated cohorts slunk back to hell bloody and bruised and said, "We are no match for Jesus. We are no match for a praying mother. We cannot penetrate the blood of Jesus." The shame they tried to put on you is now on them. He who is forgiven much loves much. God will cause all things to work together for your good. Gratitude, humility, and dependence on God daily are keys to discovering your God-given destiny.

RISING STRONG™ PROCESS
(BRENÈ BROWN, 2015)

Book one is finished: The Reckoning. The struggles and their outcome of jail, and now Adult/Teen Challenge, comprise the Reckoning. That is owning your stories of falling down, screwing up, and facing hurt so you can integrate those stories into your life and write a daring new ending.

Book two has begun: The Rumble. There at Adult/Teen Challenge, you will get honest about the stories you have made up about your struggles, and you will revisit, challenge, and reality-check the things you have believed about yourself as you dig in to topics like boundaries, shame, blame, resentment, heartbreak, generosity, and forgiveness. Rumbling with these topics and moving from our first responses to a deeper understanding of our thoughts, feelings, and behaviors gives birth to key learnings about who we are and how we engage with others. The rumble is where wholeheartedness is cultivated, and change begins.

Book three is coming: The Revolution. Revolutionary change fundamentally transforms our thoughts and beliefs. Rumbling with your story and owning your truth in order to write a new, more courageous ending transforms who you are (keeping the good stuff and casting off the bad stuff) and determines how you will manage in the real world. Through this Rising Strong™ process, those who integrate what they learn emerge into stronger people and are capable at loving, leading, parenting, and participating as productive citizens. (Brenè Brown, 2015)

Love you forever and always,

Mom

CHAPTER
7

BOUNDARIES

*Daring to set boundaries is about having the
courage to love ourselves, even when
we risk disappointing others.*
~ Brené Brown

Dear Daniel,

I am so looking forward to seeing you this Thanksgiving.
I am so proud of you and thrilled at your maturing and
increasing in peace and purpose. I've been thinking about
your phone call yesterday saying that your dad wants to pick
you up Friday after Thanksgiving, take you to Waco, and
then return you to Adult/Teen Challenge on Saturday. I am
concerned; I think that is not a good idea. Of course, I would
love to see you have a good relationship with your dad, but
there are other things to consider. You cannot put yourself in
a situation to violate your probation. I too want to believe the
best, but we cannot be naïve. I suggest that he come to Dallas
to spend a few hours with you here. You cannot put yourself
at risk of violating your probation. I don't think you should
ride in a car with him or go to his house. I know you want to

believe he is doing okay, but the reality is that he is probably still using, still struggling with explosive rage, and frankly, still not safe to be with.

If he is doing better, he will understand this and make the effort to come and see you here. It is naïve to think "nothing will happen." Do not forget the angry outbursts and fighting that you and he suffered. My last communication with him was evidence that he is still not reasonable. He sent vile and crazy texts to me that were scary.

You can build a decent relationship with him over time only if you set healthy boundaries around yourself and only if he truly has gotten help for his addictions and his rage. Be patient. One crazy episode with him could jeopardize all the good progress you have made. Be patient. Don't be naïve. Hope for the best, but don't trust him until he earns that trust over time. One kind phone call with him is not enough evidence that he is safe to be around. Trust is earned back little by little over time.

You don't know but a fraction of the things he put you and me through. I hesitate to tell you more. It is not my intent to dampen your hopes that he could be a decent father to you. I hope he can someday. But the reality is, that is not likely. He has forty years of drug abuse, explosive rage, and violence against every woman in his life, and he has never done anything unselfishly. He only does things to manipulate others to get something from them. His "kindness" has an ulterior motive. Don't be fooled. I was many times. I wanted to believe the best, until he nearly killed me. He cannot be trusted. If there is real change, he will be willing to earn back trust over time.

I know a son always longs for his father's approval and affirmation. Many sons have derailed their lives trying desperately to get from their fathers what those fathers are incapable of giving. Don't make that mistake. Find good men in your life who are healthy and willing to pour good things into you. You are not destined to be "less" because your dad is not able to be a good father. The hard fact is you cannot save him. You cannot be "good enough" to get him to give you what you need. It is not your responsibility nor is it possible for you to help him be better. Let go of the burden of wanting to fix him. Let go of the naïve longing that only he can affirm your worth.

Your relationship with him needs to be wise, with compassion but with firm, healthy boundaries. He does not define you. Your freedom will come when you can love him and grieve for his suffering, but with your eyes wide open, no longer like a child, but now as a man who can discern the truth. This will set you free, free to be all God created you to be, nothing lacking, nothing missing, nothing broken. You will know joy, peace, purpose, compassion, self-control, and wisdom for living. You control your destiny. You have free will. You choose to be wise, to confront false beliefs, and face the truth—even when it is hard. You cannot change what you refuse to acknowledge. I could not change your dad. You can't either. I stayed too long and very nearly sacrificed my life trying to love him to wholeness. It's that free will thing. If he ever changes, it will be very evident. The hard truth is that he has never acknowledged or apologized for abusing me, for abandoning you; in fact, he is still doing it.

Trust is earned over time, through consistent trustworthy behavior. So, be wise. Cry over the heartbreak, but then let it go. Do not let it define you. You are an adult now. You choose the kind of man you want to be. You choose where to put your trust. Be wise. Put your trust only in those who have earned your trust over time.

Don't hate him. Forgive him. Pray for him. But do not allow his illness, his hardness, his abandonment to influence you. Visit him in a safe place, then move on. Spend your time, focus, and energy on your life.

My hope is that you will respect my hard-won wisdom in this matter. I love you forever and always, Daniel. You are an amazing son and my heart is full, rejoicing over your growth in wisdom, respect for yourself and others, and desire to know the immense power of God in your life. He is the way, the truth, and the life. Who would say no to this extraordinary truth? My prayer is that you do not live beneath your calling but instead come to the fullness of Him who loves you and is working out His unimaginable, beautiful, plan for your life. Seek His will in all you do. Surrender all to His lordship. Let him mold you into the real you. Only He can show you who you are and why you are here. Don't settle for less than His best.

Wholeheartedly for you always,
Mom

UNINTENDED CONSEQUENCES

Daniel was hurt and angry with me for saying these things in this letter about his dad. It was not my intention to criticize and judge his dad. My heart still grieves over his struggles. I grieve over my inadequacy to help him. I cannot imagine the suffering that the stronghold of addiction has over a man. I hate addiction. The pain and suffering, the grief, the feeling of impotence to break it must be horrendous. Too many fathers, mothers, husbands, brothers, and sisters have been stolen from their families by this insidious evil.

Although I believe I have come a long way toward healing through forgiving and through facing my own failures, reading this letter again reveals that pain, loss, and a bit of anger are still resident in me. May I learn to love with deep compassion for those who are struggling, those who are lonely and lost. May that dark place in me that judges another be forever banished from my soul. May I have the courage to face my own demons. May I lean into my own distortions, my own self-righteousness, my own brokenness to shine the light of Christ's love there, that deep compassion replaces the darkness.

BUT WE STILL NEED BOUNDARIES

The truth still is that we need healthy boundaries. How do we love sincerely yet protect ourselves from toxic relationships? Some call it tough love. One healthy boundary is to learn not to get sucked into another person's drama. It is difficult to be around people who are easily offended. Through their own unresolved pain, unwillingness to forgive, and unregenerate spirit, they can suck the life out of you. Knowing when not to answer the phone or when not to respond to an insult can save you from agonizing and unnecessary strife. Sometimes it comes from our own immediate family. The boundary is still necessary.

I have a brother, Steve, who has been lost in addiction to alcohol for over thirty years. He lives on the streets in Dallas. I love him so much. He is nine years younger than I am, and he has always had a special place in my heart. He has beautiful blue eyes, and when he is in his right mind, he is kind, funny, and compassionate. Alcohol has almost completely stolen his sanity. I've tried to help him many times, and it always ended badly. He called our father last week and asked to speak with me. I reluctantly took the call. I told him I loved him and asked how he was doing. He ranted profanities, accusations, and blasted me for ten minutes as I listened silently. I love him still but finally hung up the phone. I cannot allow him in my house anymore.

Every time I see a homeless person, I think of Steve out there under a bridge and give them food or money and hope someone will show mercy to Steve. The grief is sometimes too much to bear, so I must take captive my thoughts, do what I can, and continue to serve where I am called. I do not understand why Steve rejects help. The invitation is always there. We have begged him to go to Mercy House or Adult/Teen Challenge, but he refuses. I am thankful for the Salvation Army who has reached out to him several times. I am thankful for the county hospital that has saved his life many times. His twin sister, Sue, and all our family intercede for him and long for the day he will come home. Steve's saga has been and continues to be excruciating for our mother. Sometimes I drive by the homeless camps here in Dallas and scan under the highway bridges looking for him.

If you are coming out of addiction, it is essential to set healthy boundaries. It is so true that you cannot return to the same friends or the same places where you were bound. Get strong yourself. Build a skill set that is impenetrable before attempting to help those yet bound. You cannot give away what you do not have. You become like the people you associate with. Nurture healthy relationships. Find others who are seeking freedom. It takes courage to do that. Do it anyway. Your life depends on it. Your freedom and your purpose are tied to those you might not yet know. Pursue freedom and your purpose with all your intention. Others are depending on you to get free and be that lifeline for them.

CHAPTER
8

PRESENCE

*A thin place is a place where heaven and earth come
very close. Time has a way of losing its urgency.
There is peace in a thin place. Often, we stumble
upon thin places as they unexpectedly, gently
rescue us from hustle and invites us to just breathe
and experience being loved, connected, free,
unencumbered— like a warm blanket in front
of a cozy fire with nowhere else to be,
nothing else to do.*

~ Deb Yoder

Perfect peace. Those words gently resonate within me as I pull the covers up to my chin and roll over to snuggle into the warm spot in my bed. Perfect peace. I hear it again, gently whispered but clearly important. The words come from within me and all around me. I don't "think" of it; instead, the words are just there as a precious gift placed by love itself on the foot of my bed.

It is 6:30 in the morning. The house is quiet. Now sitting in my favorite chair, sipping the first cup of coffee of the morning, I can barely hear a train in the distance. I remember a scripture I read many years ago: "You keep me in perfect peace when my mind is stayed on You." How would life be if more moments were bathed in perfect peace?

"Peace I leave with you not as the world gives but as I give." Those words gently float across my mind leaving their caress lingering sweetly in the air I breathe. Each breath feels like nourishment to my thirsty soul. It's in each breath. For a moment my thoughts attempt to distract me, pulling me to the things I need to "do" today. I resist. To be in this moment, this place of perfect peace is far more delightful than any other thought. It is a calm delight.

Every morning, for as long as I can remember, my first waking thoughts contained a sense of urgency. *Get up! You have lots to do. You are behind in preparing for your upcoming classes. You still haven't written that report that should have been done weeks ago. And, oh yeah, how in the world are you going to pay all these bills . . . how, with all the debt you are already under? Are you sure about what you're doing anyway? Get up! Get busy! You have to figure all this stuff out!*

It occurs to me now, as the steam tickles my nose as I sip on my second cup of coffee: just breathe. The answers are not in, "Get up! Get busy! Do something!" The answers are in the stillness, in this quiet, effortless being, in being fully present in this moment, now.

As a teacher of mindfulness, it has become my practice to start my mornings slowly, to set my intention to be aware, present, and peaceful throughout the day. No matter how many years I have been engaged in formation work, in all my heartfelt attempts to live undivided, I shouldn't be surprised that I'm still frequently tested. This morning was one of those pop quizzes the Universe sends to keep me humble.

As I listen to calming music on the hour drive to campus, I feel well prepared for my 9:30 psychology class. Today's topic is consciousness, one of my favorites, because it gives me the opportunity to share practical insights that may help my students experience life with less anxiety, a dose of self-compassion, and empathy for others. My outline is ready, along with an interactive PowerPoint with relevant video clips. The bumper-to-bumper traffic doesn't upset me. I happily let other drivers merge into my lane. Once parked, I stroll to my office, appreciative that the Texas heat has subsided, and the trees are wearing their stunning fall colors.

Poised and still quite peaceful, I walk mindfully to the classroom where a hundred eager young minds wait. Then, here comes the test of my intention. The computer does not work. The projector does not work. The audio does not work. I remain calm, trying the fixes that usually remedy the problems, but to no avail, and I finally call the tech support office. I get the answering machine.

Still fairly peaceful, I put the students in learning groups and offer some initial questions for them to discuss. Then I head to the tech support office. That's when the inner dialogue begins: *Come on already! This is like the fifth time this semester that nothing works. I take a few more strides. How come nobody answered the phone? If they had answered, I could have stayed with my class.*

I knock loudly on the office door. When no one responds, I go in and hunt for someone. I find a young man who appears annoyed that I have interrupted him enjoying his breakfast taco.

I try my best to be polite as I ask for help. He follows me to the classroom, tinkers with the computer, and within minutes blurts out, "It ain't happenin' today."

I hear myself reply, "Thank you for trying. Perhaps you can fix it before my next class on Thursday." In my head another script runs, *Come on, buddy! This is your job!*

As the techie leaves the room, I return to my lesson on awareness. I know my body language and my unintentional scowl belie my "acceptance" of a change of plans. I stop mid-sentence, look my students in the eyes, and say, "Let's really practice awareness. What am I feeling right now?"

Without hesitation, a normally reserved student says, "Frustrated!" Another adds, "Disappointed." A third, more forthright voice offers, "You're pissed!"

"Okay. So now that you are aware, and I am aware of this negative emotion, what's the grown-up thing to do here?"

The test that confronted me that day turns into the lesson. I ask my students for suggestions to problem-solve this situation. A shy baseball player says, "Just send us the links to the videos." The class applauds his great idea. Others chime in, "Just breathe, Dr. Yoder. We like your stories better anyway." We laugh. I say aloud, "I'm not mad anymore." They know already. We laugh again.

That day, my students learned that unrecognized and uncontrolled emotion can lead us to hurt others or engage in irrational behavior. Rather than employing our more rational minds to solve problems, we behave like undisciplined toddlers, throwing fits, sulking, or demanding revenge. Simply becoming aware of our emotional state and naming it out loud has the phenomenal effect of diminishing its control over us.

Unfortunately, to the detriment of others and ourselves, we often replay a perceived injustice over and over until a slight becomes a storm in our minds.

"If we can see the story we are in when we fall into our various compulsive behaviors and moods, then we might know how to move through them more freely and with less distress."
~ Thomas Moore, *Care of the Soul*[24]

Parker Palmer teaches that the journey toward an undivided life, a life of wholeness, requires facing our shadow and light. The challenge in the classroom that day caused me to think, feel, and do things contrary to who I am and how I want to show up in the world. Perhaps it was my shadow showing up as ego, that darker self-centered, self-important imposter that prevents me from being present, empathic, and peaceful.

When I recounted the morning's events, a colleague reminded me that we all have a story. The tech office had recently lost a long-time team member to cancer. The guy who came to my class was dealing with his own health issues in addition to being overwhelmed by the loss of his friend.

What followed was shame. How do I now get loose from shame? I recognize it just as I do other emotions. Name it, resolve to choose compassion, consider the others' perspective, and let it go. Such a process requires forgiving myself and if I have harmed another, asking for her or his forgiveness. It also requires self-compassion.

"If we are able to stay with our frustrations long enough and not give up, we may begin to suspect that the things that most need to be known and solved and figured out in our life are not going to be discovered, solved or figured out at the thinking level anyway. The things we most need to know, solve and figure out will be heard at the listening level, that place within us where God's spirit witnesses with our pirit. Here God speaks to us of things that cannot be understood through human wisdom or shuffled around and filed away in the mind. Spiritual discernment is given as pure gift in God's way, in God's time, beyond what the human mind can force."

~ Ruth Haley Barton, *Invitation to Solitude and Silence*[25]

It's a lesson of which I need to be periodically reminded, and one I trust my students took with them from that class. In the midst of life's small frustrations and major challenges, we can pause and become aware of a thin place inside ourselves. A place of calmness, wholeness, and peace. A place from which we can make better choices and take creative action. A place where heaven and earth come very close. Time has a way of losing its urgency. There is peace.

Often, we stumble upon thin places as they unexpectedly, gently rescue us from the hustle and invite us to just breathe and experience being loved, connected, free, unencubered— like a being wrapped in a warm blanket in front of a cozy fire with nowhere else to be, nothing else to do.

Such places even show up in the classroom, gracing us with life's energy, empowering us to listen deeply and love well, and enabling us to be who we want to be.

NEW BEGINNINGS FOR MOM

Now that Daniel is in a safe place, and I am intentional about practicing presence, I realized that I have lots more time, energy, and money. Becoming increasingly restless, not knowing what to do with myself, I decided to reread some old journals. I had seriously forgotten what I liked, what I wanted to do, and had even neglected a measure of self-care. So, I signed up for piano lessons and guitar lessons, and took up golf again. Oh my, life was fun again. That is when I met Byron. There was finally room in my life for love. I had been single for twenty years. I was perfectly content in my single-ness . . . most of the time. But now, oh my, Byron seems like the real deal. Can I trust myself again? Can I trust him?

By December, we were married. We sold our respective houses and moved out of the city into a home that could accommodate our aging parents as well as provide a refuge for the two of us. Byron considers Daniel as his own son and has spoken much wisdom into his life. I sometimes wonder where this man was fifteen years ago when I really needed help with Daniel. Byron and I realize that we both were on a journey of awakening to our true selves and healing during that time. We continue to learn how to live in the present moment, to stop ruminating about the past, and to stop worrying about the future. His favorite saying is, "We are okay today."

When we learn to listen to ourselves and who we are, finally, the whole of our life begins to make sense. *"Every single thing that didn't make sense when it happened, that seemed too harsh or too random or too shameful, now finds its place in the storyline that brought us here."* (Ruth Haley Barton) So, how do we learn, or re-learn, to listen to that still, small voice that you recognize as your own, that affirms who you are and reveals the purpose and meaning for your life? I want what I do to flow from me like a river, no forcing and no holding back. A river doesn't struggle to flow. It just flows. It's in its nature. I want what I do to flow out of the essence of my being. First to be, then to do.

It first requires shutting out all the noise. It is first a call to quiet. Be still and know. This is a skill, a discipline, and a practice that can be learned. The irony is that if we fail to make time to be still and quiet, life has a way of forcing it on us. The body may be the smartest part of us. It will eventually tell you loudly and clearly that it is tired, worn out, and on the verge of rebellion. We get sick and unable to continue at our usual frantic pace, hustling for worthiness. When we fail to rest, we do violence to our souls.

Resting is counter-cultural. A litany of voices demands that we constantly hustle. If you are not mindful and aware of these harsh task masters that scream at us to be productive, be in a hurry, to do more, then they are in control and you are not. Here is another irony: a leisurely pace accomplishes more than hurried striving. When I rush, I forget who I am. So then, the call is to recognize the voices. What are they saying? Is it true? Is it just? Are the messages calling us to be present, connected, and joyful? Or are they saying, "You are not enough. You are so far behind. You are not doing enough." Or worse, are they saying, "You blew it. You don't deserve to be happy. You will never be enough." Left unchecked, these voices, whether they are coming from your own inner dialogue or from someone else, can lead to depression, exhaustion, anxiety, or suicidal thoughts. Words are so very powerful. Life and death are in words. Speak life.

PART 3
BECOMING WISE
Teach me how to do Life

CHAPTER
9

SPIRITUAL FORMATION

Spiritual formation is for everyone. Just as there is an 'outer you' that is being formed and shaped all the time, like it or not, by accident or on purpose, so there is an 'inner you.' You have a spirit. And it's constantly being shaped and tugged at: by what you hear and watch and say and read and think and experience.

~ John Ortberg

To create a life you love, one that is fulfilling and of service to others, requires intentional practices. As I said earlier, I was twenty-nine before I began to understand that we are body, soul, and spirit. We are tripartite beings. We are called to walk in the spirit, that is, relying on the Holy Spirit of God to renew our minds and produce the kind of life that produces good fruit. Ignoring or denying this truth causes us to live out of our unregenerate flesh. Denying the existence of or being ignorant of the real you—your spirit—and then trying to be or do better is simply a behavior modification program.

You simply exchange chaos for legalism. It does not work. However, when we learn to trust in and rely on the Spirit of Truth to will and to work in us, and we set our intention to cooperate, then lasting transformation can happen.

It is also helpful to realize that your mind is not your brain. When we try to live from intellect alone, we fall way short. Now, in my sixties, I marvel and grieve that we don't teach about the most important part of us: the real, sacred, eternal us, our spirit. In school, we only focus on developing the brain and perhaps our bodies with physical education. I never took a course in spiritual education. I didn't even know I had a spirit!

Corrie Ten Boom (1892-1983) endured unspeakable suffering in Ravensbruck concentration camp during World War II. Her faith sustained her even after losing her father, brother, and sister to the brutality of their captors. Surviving the Holocaust, Corrie traveled the world with the message of reconciliation. She knew well through experiential knowledge that "trying to do the Lord's work in your own strength is the most confusing, exhausting, and tedious of all work. But when you are filled with the Holy Spirit, then the ministry of Jesus just flows out of you."[26]

Renovaré[27] Institutes provides a helpful explanation of what spiritual formation is all about:

> "We are all spiritual beings. We have physical bodies, but our lives are largely driven by an unseen part of us. There is an immaterial center in us that shapes the way we see the world and ourselves, directs the choices we make, and guides our actions. Our spirit is the most

important part of who we are. And yet we rarely spend time developing our inner life. That's what Spiritual Formation is all about."

Spiritual Formation is a process, but it is also a journey through which we open our hearts to a deeper connection with God. We are not bystanders in our spiritual lives; we are active participants with God, who is ever inviting us into relationship with Him. Jesus said, "I came that they may have life and have it abundantly" (John 10:10). This abundant life is possible. So, why do so many live far short of this truth?

Why is Spiritual Formation Important?

Closeness with God brings us true freedom and fullness (John. 8:36, Colossians 2:9-10). Yet many people—Christians included—find their lives fall short of the kind Jesus promised and proclaimed. If God is present with us, why is there so little joy, power, energy, and peace in our lives?

We keep trying to find happiness, to experience God, to fill the emptiness. And that's the problem. Trying just tires us out, distracts us from what's important, and discourages us when we fail.

We are eternal beings but have lost sight of eternal living. We spend time, energy, and money on our physical needs, but neglect our souls. Our misplaced efforts leave us feeling powerless and detached from God.

That's not how God intended it to be. We are meant to be in relationship with God and others in a way that is dynamic, whole, and fresh every day (John 17:24, 2 Corinthians 4:16)

—a relationship that extends beyond church services into every facet of our lives.

Spiritual Formation helps us reclaim our relationship with God as it was meant to be. It's not trying—it's training in eternal living, determined discipleship to Jesus Christ, and the way we discover the renewable source of spiritual energy we've been looking for (2 Corinthians 4:16)."

Dear Daniel,

The life lessons you will learn at Adult/Teen Challenge this year, and as you pursue wisdom for the rest of your life, will give you keys to your identity and ultimately to help others create a life they love with very real peace, passion, and purpose.

I wish I had begun the process of pursuing wisdom for living at your age. The good news is that the moment we choose to pursue wisdom, the process begins, and life immediately gets better. And when tough times do come, you have the wisdom to walk through them without getting knocked off your horse. Even if you get knocked down on occasion, you will know how to get back up.

Wholeheartedly for You,

Mom

RESOURCES FOR SPIRITUAL FORMATION

So many people have seen misrepresentations of who God really is. People claiming to be Christians have badgered and manipulated others through guilt and condemnation. No wonder people reject the Gospel! They have not truly seen the true gospel. Well, I reject "that gospel" too. My brother, David, had a friend that would get furious if you brought up anything spiritual. The mention of the name Jesus would send him into a rage. He posted a picture on Facebook asserting there was a 100% chance that he would never 'give his life to Jesus.' I don't blame him, for the 'Jesus' presented to him was not accurate. Much damage is done with catastrophic consequences, often for generations, by this misrepresentation of the Gospel. The insidious lie is especially unfortunate because those who are deceived do not know they are deceived. There are churches full of people who think they have it right. They have heard a fire-escape gospel, that is, say this prayer to invite Jesus into your heart, then you will be saved. First, how can they do that unless they are drawn by love? And, how can they live the kingdom life if there is no mention of what next?

I said 'the sinner's prayer' several times, once as an eight-year-old kid, again in high school, but not much changed. It was not until I came to the end of myself and had a heart change that my prayer was sincere. As long as I was on the throne of my life, transformation was not welcome. I, in no means, want to imply that saying the 'sinner's prayer' is impotent. Millions have responded to an invitation to do just that and transformation began immediately. But I had a hard heart. It took years of chastening, often crushing me to powder, for me to look up, helpless, and truly say from that place of brokenness, "Son of David, have mercy on me, a sinner." I didn't say it quite like that back then; I said, "God, if you are there, take my life and do something good with it because all I see is blackness."

I then wanted to learn about the One Who said He would save me, (although I had no idea what "save" meant), the One Who would replace my heart of stone with a willing, humble heart. The One Who wanted to teach me wisdom and give me a life of joy, purpose, and excellence. So, I went to a church near my apartment. It was a small Baptist church and for a year I attended regularly, searched for answers and began reading the Bible. The Bible made no sense to me. I could not understand much of anything. After one year, I was driving home across the bridge after an evening service very disillusioned. I beat the steering wheel and shouted, "If this is all there is to Christianity, you can have it!" In that particular church, Sunday after Sunday, I heard the same message of salvation. We sang the first and third stanzas of "Just as I Am" and nervously waited to see if anyone would walk down the aisle to the front. I loved God and wanted to grow. I went home and called my sister, Sue. I told her what I had done while driving across the bridge. She said,

"Deb, I want to tell you about the Holy Spirit."

"Sue, please tell me all you know! I am desperate to know if this God thing is real!"

Sue suggested I read Acts 19. "While Apollos was at Corinth, Paul took the road through the interior and arrived at Ephesus. There he found some disciples [2] and asked them, 'Did you receive the Holy Spirit when you believed?'

They answered, 'No, we have not even heard that there is a Holy Spirit.'

[3]So Paul asked, 'Then what baptism did you receive?'

'John's baptism,' they replied.

I had been water baptized in that church but attending for over a year, I never heard about the Holy Spirit. At first, I was angry because in my immature thinking, I thought they were keeping something from me. Later, I realized that they did not know the truth of the Holy Spirit either. How very important it is to seek God for yourself. Yes, seek wise counsel but question what you are being taught.

My husband, Byron, was active in a non-denominational Bible church for thirty-three years, serving many of those years as Chairman of the Deacon board. He never heard teaching on the Holy Spirit either. When his marriage imploded after thirty-three years, he went to the pastoral team. They had no idea his marriage was in trouble. Their response was yelling condemnation, issuing ultimatums, and expressing great concern over how this would make the church look. They forbade him from taking communion. Byron never went back.

Instead he immersed himself in the book of Romans and its message of freedom: freedom from sin, freedom to enter God's eternal kingdom, freedom to know Jesus Christ personally, and freedom from the bondage of guilt, isolation, loneliness, emptiness and legalism. He sought out a healthy, balanced, Christian counselor, and pursued God earnestly from a broken-open heart. That year of earnestly seeking God alone in his apartment transformed him. His friends and his children are astonished at the freedom in which Byron now lives. Since then, Byron devours books on kingdom living: Dallas Willard, John Ortberg, Gary Moon, Dietrich Bonhoeffer, Richard Foster, and above all—the Bible. In two years, he has listened to 90+ audio books, prays as a man who knows his God, and exemplifies the fruit of the spirit in his countenance, relationships and his business. Legalism kills. The Spirit brings freedom.

If you want to pursue that same freedom and the wisdom to live a life of peace, passion, and purpose, you may want to consider taking a look at the resources that have helped me and many others who now live their lives in victory. These have been enormously helpful, but nothing compares to you spending slow, unhurried, time pouring your heart out to God. Nothing compares to sitting quietly and yearning to hear His whisper. Faith comes by hearing. If you are hearing truth, your faith will grow in the reality of kingdom life now. If you are listening to fear, legalism, and condemnation, or a "works" message, you have an impotent faith in yourself or in a failed system. Hear truth. Speak truth. Guard your heart because out of it flow the issues of life.

RESOURCES FOR SPIRITUAL FORMATION

https://renovare.org Training over trying.
Renovaré provides practical resources for cultivating a life—the with-God life—that makes us like Jesus from the inside out.

Surrender to Love: Discovering the Heart of Christian Spirituality expanded edition by David G. Benner, InterVarsity Press, ©2015

The Divine Conspiracy: Rediscovering our Hidden Life in God by Dallas Willard, HarperCollins Publishers, ©1997

Invitation to Solitude and Silence: Experiencing God's Transforming Presence by Ruth Haley Barton, InterVarsity Press Formatio Books, 2nd edition, ©2010

The Breaking of the Outward Man for The Release of the Spirit by Watchman Nee, Christian Fellowship Publishers, Inc., ©2000

Spiritual Direction and the Care of Souls: A Guide to Christian Approaches and Practices edited by Gary Moon and David Benner, InterVarsity Press, ©2004

A Hidden Wholeness: The Journey toward an Undivided Life, Welcoming the Soul and Weaving Community in a Wounded World by Parker Palmer, Jossey-Bass, ©2004

Eternity Is Now in Session: A Radical Rediscovery of What Jesus Really Taught about Salvation, Eternity, and Getting to the Good Place by John Ortberg, Tyndale House Publishers, ©2018

Eternal Living: Reflections on Dallas Willard's Teaching on Faith and Formation edited by Gary Moon, InterVarsity Press, ©2015

Streams of Living Water: Essential Practices from the Six Great Traditions of Christian Faith by Richard J. Foster, HarperCollins, ©2001

Rising Strong: How the Ability to Reset Transforms the Way We Live, Love, Parent, and Lead by Brené Brown, Random House, ©2015

Switch on Your Brain: The Key to Peak Happiness, Thinking, and Health by Caroline Leaf, ©2013

I Declare: 31 Promises to Declare Over Your Life by Joel Osteen, ©2014

CHAPTER
10

LOVE

The things that we love tell us what we are.
~ Thomas Aquinas

My Dear Daniel,

I love you forever and always. That is a fact. God, in His wisdom, just made mothers that way. I think it is a picture of how God loves us. He loves us unconditionally, regardless of what we do. When we believe the absolute truth that He loves us, we respond by loving Him back. We don't have to earn His love. You don't have to earn my love. It just is.

When we live with the revelation that we are loved, it changes us. We want to please the One who loves. It occurred to me this morning that -- even when we rebel and go our own way relying on our own arrogance that we can do life separate from this understanding -- that love is still there waiting for us to come home.

I believe God created the family structure as a picture of the kingdom of God. He is father. We are His beloved. When we learn His ways and obey Him, life goes well. Everything in the kingdom belongs to us. He gladly gives us access to all good things. However, when we rebel and say we don't need God, our fists are clenched so we cannot receive the provisions freely offered to us, the essential things that enable us to live our lives with joy and excellence.

I've always told you that I will give you the moon if you follow the rules with a grateful heart. When you rebelled, disrespected me, and broke the rules, I had to make you leave my house because it was unlivable. I had lived in fear once before and I knew I could not do it again.

I know you were just confused and lacked understanding then. You also had unresolved hurt that wreaked havoc on your mind. I'm not blaming you or shaming you. We have all had a rebellious heart. I am so thankful that God always invites us back home. We can come back in His presence and live in His kingdom when we repent (turn from our ill-fated thinking) and humble ourselves before Him to be taught by Him how to live in His kingdom. If we truly understand the depth and power of His love, if we really understand that our true life is so incredibly powerful and joyful, with amazing purpose and meaning, we would be so hungry to know everything we could know about life in His kingdom. Kingdom is a strange word these days, but I believe it is simply God's way of being and doing things. It is another dimension. We still live in a fallen world, but our citizenship is in heaven. The Holy Spirit empowers us, counsels us, and guides us if we have ears to hear, that is, if we set our minds to seek Him with our whole heart. As much as I love you, human love is imperfect. Only God loves us with a perfect love. It requires vulnerability to trust in this perfect love. Our view of love and acceptance is tainted by our experiences of disappointment in human love. However, all love is of God. Even imperfect human love heals. It helps us to believe that we indeed have worth, are cared for, and accepted even in our brokenness. When my brother, David, was days from dying of pancreatic cancer, I knelt by his bed and gently stroked his hand for hours. In his very vulnerable state, he whispered, "I feel like I could tell you anything." Without words, my presence, loving him unconditionally invited him to let go of all performance, the imposter self, realizing he was loved even though he could do nothing to earn it. The room was filled with a peaceful presence. He whispered, "I don't know what I believe." The honesty and vulnerability of this truth, unmasked, laid bare of any pretense, completely and totally truthful, ushered in the presence of Perfect Love. We both knew we were in the presence of something more beautiful than we had ever experienced. In silence, we soaked in a light that tenderly and thoroughly washed away the world as we had known it. We were in a bubble where there was no fear, no hustling, no heartache, no cancer. The silent prayer was, "Show me what I do not know." After what seemed like forever, I whispered, "I believe in Love." David replied, "I do, too."

Believing God loves us is a good thing. Faith is good. Hope is essential. But only experiencing divine love transforms us. Experiencing perfect love draws us to deeper places of trust and intimacy, of presence and power, of wisdom and purpose.

It's taken me years to understand that this has nothing to do with religion or doctrine. In fact, religious tradition can block us from truth. It is, instead, a personal relationship with the person of Jesus Christ. I heard that for years but had no idea what it really meant. How can you have a relationship, how can you experience love, with a person you cannot see, feel, hear, or touch? I came to the end of myself and knew there had to be more to life than what I was experiencing. In exhaustion, I prayed, "God, if you are there, take my life and do something good with it." The unspoken plea was, "Show me what I do not know." I believe in that moment a great exchange took place. My heart of stone was replaced by a receptive heart. My desires changed. Humility and vulnerability opened a wide door of hope that I could learn about God. That was thirty-four years ago. However, it was only about five years ago that I came to experience a personal relationship with God. Wow.

I did grow and learn during those earlier years. I was set free from depression and anxiety. I learned what I had done wrong in relationships and learned how to have healthy relationships. I was learning to trust the unseen God. I learned to some degree what living by faith means. But I think five years ago, I became a disciple. That simply means a learner, a student, a serious seeker of the teachings of Jesus, an apprentice, not just to know it intellectually but to live out what I am learning. Experiential transformation was what I was earnestly seeking.

Becoming all of who God created you to be is not just a behavior modification program wherein if you do good, then you get good results. It is so much more than that. Of course, obedience is required, as it protects us from unwanted consequences, but take it a giant step further. Yes, you need to renew your mind by the word of God, challenge wrong thinking, let truth replace distorted beliefs, and do what the word says in order to improve the quality of your life. But that is only like graduating from high school. To live in the fullness of who you are now in Christ, to get an advanced degree, is to acknowledge, receive, and experience the very real presence of God; to ask for and receive the fullness of the Holy Spirt that empowers you to hear, see, feel, and touch the magnificence of His glory. The Bible is no longer a book of rules and condemnation. It comes alive. It is spirit and life. I believe His glory is the manifest presence of God as experienced by humans. He takes us from glory to glory. I experienced a measure of His glory when I was twenty-nine. I am now experiencing a much greater measure of His glory—His presence. This is not simply an emotional experience or mental ascent. It is real. Alone and quiet, I am in the safest, loveliest, bubble where there is no fear, no hustling, no heartache, only pure love and belonging.

When we are humble, grateful, and obedient, He gladly pours out His favor on us. Now that you are grateful and learning to make healthy decisions, I am happy to provide what you need, such as money, clothes, encouragement, etc. But when you were doing wrong things, I could not give you money or anything else. You were using my provision to do harmful things. Think of it this way: if Cora was using drugs, would you give her money? Of course not. You would not want to assist her in destroying herself. But suppose she came to you and said, "Daddy, teach me to live. Show me how to make good decisions. I'll do what you say because I trust you.

I'll be grateful if you take me in and provide for me while I learn how to live." You would gladly provide all in your power to help her. I think that is the way God is with us. When we ask for help with a humble heart and set our mind to trust and obey, He opens the windows of heaven to provide all we need. But if we are halfhearted, or hard-hearted, or insist that we are self-sufficient, He has to say no. It's not because He doesn't love you but precisely because He does love you and knows what is best for you. I believe it grieves the Holy Spirit when we go our own way, but His faithful love never fails. He is close to the brokenhearted. Draw near to God and He will draw near to you. May you know the immensity of His love for you.

Wholeheartedly for you forever,
Mom

"Finally, the whole of our life begins to make sense. Every single thing that didn't make sense when it happened, that seemed too harsh or too random or too shameful, now finds its place in the storyline that brought us here."
~ Ruth Haley Barton, *Invitation to Solitude and Silence*[28]

EPILOGUE

by Daniel Peters III & Deb Yoder

A WORD FROM DANIEL:
A LIFE OF JOY AND EXCELLENCE

I have always had the belief that everything happens for a reason, that every action and reaction is given its perfectly timed cue. It took me reaching the lowest point in my life to realize who arranges these perfect coincidences in time. The timing of God revealing His face to me was in itself an unblemished action. Everything leading up to where I am today needed to happen for me to come to the end of myself and begin to search for God's will in my life. He revealed Himself to me at the ideal time in my life and gifted me my testimony in the process. I now have the faith that God is not surprised. I believe He saw my heart and plucked me out of the pit my decisions had landed me in.

It is never a painless process to move forward. In fact, I'm finding it is continuously challenging, daily, to put one foot in front of the other and make one right decision after another towards a clear goal. My vision was cloudy in this sense until I finally realized that it is only possible to get so far on my own. Putting things into perspective and truly taking a step back and seeing what it really was, through my mind's eye, what He pulled me out of is what keeps me passionate and motivated. From the circle of negativity I was surrounding myself in, the poor choice of friends and roommates, the broken family, the cold nights sleeping in a crippled car, the streets, and to eventually a jail cell, the darkest point in the mess that I had created for myself was sitting in a cell unsure of how long I would be there and if my actions had truly cost me my future. I hold onto that moment, strictly for reference to the bottom line of my testimony: that my God is a faithful God.

When my faith seems to be shaking like a chain-link fence, that's the moment I refer back to. He pulled me out of that and gave me an opportunity to be a father to my daughter again. In that act alone, I can see His perfect love for me, and I know He gave me my testimony to share it, not to keep it for myself. Nearly two years after that moment in the cell, I can be a dad to my daughter again. I am grateful that I had the opportunity to be taken out of that situation and set aside for a year at Adult & Teen Challenge to simply focus on working to better my faults and weaknesses. I think this would have only been possible if I was focusing on God and His will in my life.

I've seen a lot of people come and go through my stay at the program. It seemed that there was a constant recurring theme distinguishing the guys that made it from the guys that chose to leave early, or even graduated, but fell off quickly after returning home. The people that had their minds made up thoroughly that they didn't want to go back to their old lives seemed to carry themselves differently and truly absorb all that they could get while they were here. It's as if you could sniff it out, the desire for a better future. On the other hand, you could tell when someone wasn't being genuine. I feel like the men that had finally come to their rock bottom and extinguished all of their resources, crying out to God, were the ones that truly saw the results and progress along the way. I made a friend named Dale during my stay at the program, and we were alike in a lot of ways, both into fitness and nutrition, both with young children, and both came to the end of ourselves in our mess and needed a change. The difference I noticed early on in our friendship was that Dale didn't seem to be all in. Where others, who were obviously invested in their walk, would worship or have an opportunity to serve someone else, you could just tell in Dale's body language and attitude that his pride was still in the way of him being able to be all the way in and fully devoted to his spiritual renovation. Sadly, Dale went home early from the program and got back involved in his drug habit and his old circle of friends, got in some trouble, and is now awaiting trial for a lengthy prison sentence.

I truly believe the reason I was shown grace and have seen my life pieced back together better than it has ever been is because I fully surrendered my pride and finally accepted the call that God has had on my life forever. God has blessed me with a clear vision for the future above all else. I graduated from the program in October 2018. Currently I have secured a great job that I enjoy working, and I rent a little place that is right on the lake near my job and my daughter. I have discovered a new joy in doing the things I'm supposed to do every day. It's a wonderful process seeing the fruit that is produced when I simply put one foot in front of the other and make good decisions one after another. I look forward to being as productive as I can be every day spiritually, physically, mentally, and as a father. My hope is that my story helps you or someone else to see that God is good and is capable of anything if you walk with Him.

A WORD FROM DEB: A HOPE AND A FUTURE

By now, you are probably wondering and hoping, along with me, "Will Daniel stay the course and continue to build a life of joy and excellence?" I am confident he will. However, like any of us, it is our daily choices, sometimes moment by moment, that determines the trajectory of our lives. There is always the risk of complacency and compromise, in doing the things we know that creates an honorable life, that can derail us. There are many signs that Daniel knows this risk well. The original graduation date from Adult/Teen Challenge was July but breaking the rules and other compromises added thirty days—twice. He then was set to graduate in September; however, he elected to delay his graduation another month because he believed God had more to teach him. He truly wanted to know what caused him to compromise. That is wisdom. Daniel was wanting to know himself and understand the temptations that so easily beset him. He wanted to be confident that when he was free and on his own, without the accountability of the program, that he would not fall back into his old ways. When he told Byron and me about his decision to stay longer, Byron told him, "I am so proud of you. Many older adults could use wisdom like that."

Daniel went into the program a skinny, confused, angry young man nineteen months ago. He now is built like a linebacker, having gained thirty pounds of muscle. He exudes a humble, peaceful, quiet confidence. His focus is on others. He is a gentle listener and others are drawn to his generous acceptance of them. He is a man like Enoch. He is a peacemaker.

A NEW CREATION

The old Daniel could not hold a job, had a poor work ethic, and got into fights over the slightest offense. The new Daniel is highly respected on his job, is up for promotion, and has emerged as a leader. He loves his work and takes pride in doing things with excellence. The old Daniel was a disaster in managing money. Six months into his stay at Adult/Teen Challenge, he wrote to me and asked me to send him Dave Ramsey's Financial Freedom teaching materials. He read it twice. Daniel now is wise in his financial life. The old Daniel expected rejection, lived in survival mode, and every day was a battle for him. The new Daniel knows that when challenges come, there is an answer and that patience, perseverance, hard work, and abiding in the reality of a God-with us assurance, that the answer will come. Lack is temporary because abundance is his portion. Confusion and questions are temporary because wisdom is available for the asking.

I am overjoyed with Daniel's desire to care of his daughter, Cora. He is patient, loving, instructive, and affectionate with her. Cora loves her daddy. Daniel is intentional about nurturing a healthy relationship with Morgen. His respect for her is evident.

My boy is back. I gaze into the same gentle eyes that melted me twenty years ago when he softly whispered, "Mom, I've got birds in my pocket."

ENDNOTES

Foreword

[1] Anne Lamott, Almost Everything: Notes on hope ©2018, Penquin Random House, LLC

Introduction

[2] Adult/Teen Challenge, https://www.teenchallengeusa.com

Chapter 1

[3] Adult/Teen Challenge, Center in Azle, Texas, https://www.teenchallengeusa.com/center/1524

[4] Marcel Proust was a French novelist, critic, and essayist best known for his monumental novel À la recherche du temps perdu, published in seven parts between 1913 and 1927.

[5] Carl Jung. (n.d.). AZQuotes.com. Retrieved August 09, 2018, from AZQuotes.com Web site: https://www.azquotes.com/quote/774565

[6] Rilke, R. M., Barrows, A., & Macy, J. (2005). *Rilke's Book of hours: Love poems to God*. New York: Riverhead Books.

[7] Ted Loder, *Guerillas of Grace: Prayers for the Battle* ©1984, 2005 by Ted Loder

[8] Center for Renewal and Wholeness in Education (CRWHE) https://www.richlandcollege.edu/cd/instruct-divisions/rlc/crwhe/pages/default.aspx

[9] Touchstones were prepared by formation facilitators with considerable help from the writings of Judy Brown, Parker

Palmer and the Dialogue Group. The Center for Renewal and Wholeness in Higher Education www.couragerenewal.org   The Center for Renewal and Wholeness in Higher Education at Richland College in Dallas, Texas, is where I received formation facilitator training. Used by permission.

Chapter 2
[10] Parker Palmer, *Let Your Life Speak* ©2000 John Wiley & Sons, Inc.
[11] Dostoevsky, Fyodor. *Crime and Punishment*. Vol. XVIII. Harvard Classics Shelf of Fiction. New York: P.F. Collier & Son, 1917; Bartleby.com, 2000.
[12] Dallas Willard, *Renovation of the Heart* ©2002 NavPress

Chapter 3
[13] Debra Yoder, *When We Dare to Listen*, TEDx MountainViewCollege 2015
[14] Thomas Merton, *New Seeds of Contemplation* © 1961 by the Abbey of Gethsemane, Inc
[15] Parker Palmer, *A Hidden Wholeness* ©2004 by John Wiley & Sons, Inc.
[16] Manning, B. *Abba's child: The cry of the heart for intimate belonging*. Expanded edition. Colorado Springs, Co: NavPress. 2002
[17] Adapted from the writings of Wayne Muller, *How Then, Shall We Live? Four Simple Questions that Reveal the Beauty and Meaning of Our Lives* ©1996

[18] Dr. Martin Luther King, Jr. "The Other America." Speech by Rev. Martin Luther King, Jr. Grosse Pointe High School - March 14, 1968. Retrieved August 9, 2018 from http://www.gphistorical.org/mlk/mlkspeech/

[19] Rogers, C., *On Becoming a Person*. New York, NY: Houghton Mifflin Harcourt Publishing. 1961

Chapter 4

[20] Caroline Leaf, *Switch on Your Brain: The Key to Peak Happiness, Thinking, and Health* ©2013

[21] Joel Osteen, *I Declare: 31 Promises to Declare Over Your Life* ©2014 by Joel Osteen

Chapter 5

[22] Brené Brown, *Rising Strong*™ ©2015. First edition. New York: Spiegel & Grau, an imprint of Random House.

[23] Brené Brown, *Rising Strong*™ ©2015. First edition. New York: Spiegel & Grau, an imprint of Random House.

Chapter 8

[24] Thomas Moore, *Care of the Soul*©1992, page 12

[25] Ruth Haley Barton, *Invitation to Solitude and Silence: Experiencing God's Transforming Presence*, 2nd edition ©2010

Chapter 9

[26] Corrie ten Boom, https://www.elijahnotes.com/corrie-ten-boom-quotes/

[27] Renovare. Retrieved August 09, 2018, from https://renovare.org

Chapter 10

28 Ruth Haley Barton, *Invitation to Solitude and Silence: Experiencing God's Transforming Presence*, 2nd edition ©2010

Acknowledgments

This story may be Daniel's and mine but there is a huge cast of those who made this story possible. Thank you to my sister, Susan, who lives a life of faith that is real and without pretense that drew me to finally lay down my resistance to the idea of a God who is love and ever present.

To my sister, Linda, who has always been my tireless encourager and one of the most resilient people I know. To my brother, David, who taught me what unconditional love really looks like. To my parents, Len and Hazel, who by example, showed me how to overcome life's challenges to create a life I love.

Thank you to Bill and Jane Robinson who have loved me to wholeness, which was not an easy thing to do, and took over forty years! Thank you to Pat and Jenny Tracy, who show me how to live with quietness and grace. Thank you to Brenda Ramsey, who lived much of the story with me, saw me at my weakest and ugliest, but always loved me.

Thank you to the thousands of students over the past forty years who have allowed me to speak into their lives and only sometimes get it right. I have learned far more from you, from witnessing your courage, than you ever learned from me.

Thank you, Judge Holmes, for showing mercy to Daniel. Your decision changed the course of history. Truly, mercy triumphed over judgment.

Thank you to David Wilkerson and Adult/Teen Challenge. Your work is life-changing, bringing redemption and restoration to so many who were without hope.

Sincere gratitude to my husband, Byron Gillory, Jr., who stayed after me to complete this manuscript. Without his belief in me and his constant reminders of who I am, this work will have never been accomplished.

Thank you to Markay Rister for your excellent editing and for your encouragement along the way.

Thank you, Jeanye Mercer, for teaching me to live with grace, courage, vulnerability, and to forgive myself. Your words, your art, your laughter, and your grace lift me when I forget who I am.

And, thank you to Brené Brown and The Daring Way™ Facilitator Training, and Parker Palmer, Sue Jones, and Elaine Sullivan of the Center for Renewal and Wholeness in Higher Education. You helped me find my voice and gave me the courage to teach.

ABOUT THE AUTHOR

Deb Yoder is a psychology professor and licensed professional counselor. She earned her doctorate at the University of Texas at Austin and has masters' degrees in counseling and kinesiology. Deb is a Certified Daring Way™ Clinician, a Formation Facilitator, and an Appreciative Inquiry Facilitator—all of which are skill sets designed to help others discover who they were born to be and what they were born to do—and do it in a state of flow rather than struggle. Deb lives with her husband Byron Gillory in Rockwall, Texas where she is in private practice and facilitates formation retreats.

She can be contacted at deb@drdebyoder.com

www.twitter.com/drdebyoder
www.facebook.com/drdebyoder
www.instagram.com/drdebyoder

Made in the USA
Coppell, TX
03 May 2020